The World Wide Web
Illustrated

The World Wide Web
Illustrated

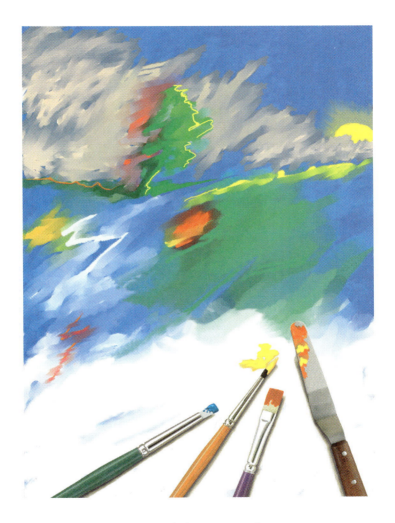

Donald I. Barker
Gonzaga University

Chia-Ling H. Barker
Spokane Falls Community College

Course Technology, Inc. One Main Street, Cambridge, MA 02142

An International Thomson Publishing Company

Albany • Bonn • Boston • Cincinnati • London • Madrid • Melbourne • Mexico City
New York • Paris • San Francisco • Singapore • Tokyo • Toronto • Washington

The World Wide Web — Illustrated is published by Course Technology, Inc.

Managing Editors:	Mac Mendelsohn, Marjorie Hunt
Senior Product Manager:	Nicole Jones Pinard
Developmental Editor:	Kim T.M. Crowley
Production Editor:	Nancy Ray
Text Designer:	Leslie Hartwell
Cover Designer:	John Gamache

© 1995 Course Technology, Inc.
A Division of International Thomson Publishing, Inc.

For more information contact:
Course Technology, Inc.
One Main Street
Cambridge, MA 02142

International Thomson Publishing Europe
Berkshire House 168-173
High Holborn
London WCIV 7AA
England

International Thomson Publishing GmbH
Königswinterer Strasse 418
53227 Bonn
Germany

Thomas Nelson Australia
102 Dodds Street
South Melbourne, 3205
Victoria, Australia

International Thomson Publishing Asia
211 Henderson Road
#05-10 Henderson Building
Singapore 0315

Nelson Canada
1120 Birchmount Road
Scarborough, Ontario
Canada M1K 5G4

International Thomson Publishing Japan
Hirakawacho Kyowa Building, 3F
2-2-1 Hirakawacho
Chiyoda-ku, Tokyo 102
Japan

International Thomson Editores
Campos Eliseos 385, Piso 7
Col. Polanco
11560 Mexico D.F. Mexico

Trademarks

Course Technology and the open book logo are registered trademarks of Course Technology, Inc.

I(T)P   The ITP logo is a trademark under license.

Some of the product names in this book have been used for identification purposes only and may be trademarks or registered trademarks of their respective manufacturers and sellers.

Disclaimer

Course Technology, Inc. reserves the right to revise this publication and make changes from time to time in its content without notice.

ISBN 0-7600-3504-0

Printed in the United States of America

10 9 8 7 6 5 4 3 2 1

From the Publisher

At Course Technology, Inc., we believe that technology will transform the way that people teach and learn. We are very excited about bringing you, college professors and students, the most practical and affordable technology-related products available.

The Course Technology Development Process

Our development process is unparalleled in the higher education publishing industry. Every product we create goes through an exacting process of design, development, review, and testing.

Reviewers give us direction and insight that shape our manuscripts and bring them up to the latest standards. Every manuscript is quality tested. Students whose backgrounds match the intended audience work through every keystroke, carefully checking for clarity, and pointing out errors in logic and sequence. Together with our own technical reviewers, these testers help us ensure that everything that carries our name is error-free and easy to use.

Course Technology Products

We show both *how* and *why* technology is critical to solving problems in college and in whatever field you choose to teach or pursue. Our time-tested, step-by-step instructions provide unparalleled clarity. Examples and applications are chosen and crafted to motivate students.

The Course Technology Team

This book will suit your needs because it was delivered quickly, efficiently, and affordably. In every aspect of business, we rely on a commitment to quality and the use of technology. Every employee contributes to this process. The names of all our employees are listed below. Diana Armington, Tim Ashe, Sara Ballestero, Debora Barrow, Stephen M. Bayle, Ann Marie Buconjic, Jody Buttafoco, Kerry Cannell, Jei Lee Chong, Jim Chrysikos, Barbara Clemens, Susan Collins, John M. Connolly, Myrna D'Addario, Lisa D'Alessandro, Jodi Davis, Howard S. Diamond, Kathryn Dinovo, Jennifer Dolan, Joseph B. Dougherty, Patti Dowley, Laurie Duncan, Karen Dwyer, MaryJane Dwyer, Kristin Dyer, Chris Elkhill, Don Fabricant, Ronan Fagan, Dean Fossella, Jane Fraser, Viktor Frengut, Jeff Goding, Laurie Gomes, Eileen Gorham, Chris Greacen, Catherine Griffin, Kathy Griffin, Jamie Harper, Roslyn Hooley, Marjorie Hunt, Matt Kenslea, Marybeth LaFauci, Susannah Lean, Kim Mai, Margaret Makowski, Tammy Marciano, Elizabeth Martinez, Debbie Masi, Don Maynard, Kathleen McCann, Sarah McLean, Jay McNamara, Mac Mendelsohn, Karla Mitchell, Kim Munsell, Michael Ormsby, Debbie Parlee, Kristin Patrick, Darren Perl, Kevin Phaneuf, Nicole Jones Pinard, Nancy Ray, Brian Romer, Carla Sharpe, Deborah Shute, Roger Skilling, Jennifer Slivinski, Christine Spillett, Audrey Tortolani, Michelle Tucker, David Upton, Jim Valente, Mark Valentine, Renee Walkup, Tracy Wells, Donna Whiting, Rob Williams, Janet Wilson, Lisa Yameen.

Preface

Course Technology, Inc. is proud to present this new book in its Illustrated series. *The World Wide Web — Illustrated* provides a highly visual, hands-on introduction to the World Wide Web. The book is designed as a learning tool for Web and Netscape novices but will also be useful as a source for future reference.

Organization and Coverage

The World Wide Web — Illustrated contains a Windows overview and five units that cover basic Web skills. In these units students learn how to use Netscape to navigate, search, and explore the Web. Students also learn how to create their own Web page. This book also includes a valuable appendix on other Internet resources.

Approach

The World Wide Web — Illustrated distinguishes itself from other textbooks with its highly visual approach to computer instruction.

Lessons: Information Displays

The basic lesson format of this text is the "information display," a two-page lesson that is sharply focused on a specific task. This sharp focus and the precise beginning and end of a lesson make it easy for students to study specific material. Modular lessons are less overwhelming for students, and they provide instructors with more flexibility in planning classes and assigning specific work.

Each lesson, or "information display," contains the following elements:

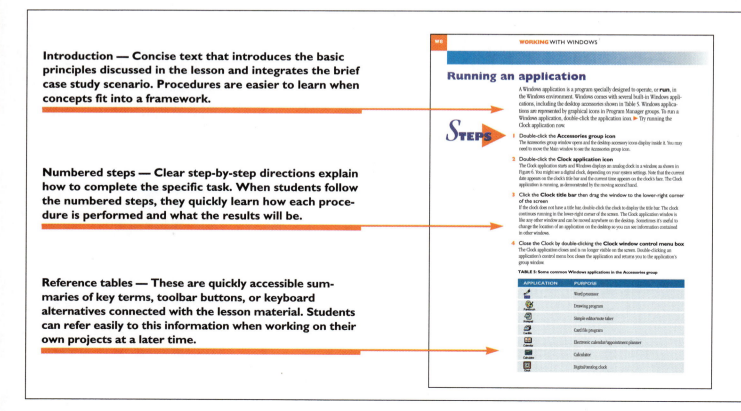

Introduction — Concise text that introduces the basic principles discussed in the lesson and integrates the brief case study scenario. Procedures are easier to learn when concepts fit into a framework.

Numbered steps — Clear step-by-step directions explain how to complete the specific task. When students follow the numbered steps, they quickly learn how each procedure is performed and what the results will be.

Reference tables — These are quickly accessible summaries of key terms, toolbar buttons, or keyboard alternatives connected with the lesson material. Students can refer easily to this information when working on their own projects at a later time.

Features

The World Wide Web — Illustrated is an exceptional textbook because it contains the following features:

- "Read This Before You Begin" pages — These pages, one for the Windows section and one before Unit 1, provide essential information that both students and instructors need to know before they begin working through the units.

- Windows Overview — The "Working with Windows" section provides an overview so students can begin working in the Windows environment right away. This section introduces students to the graphical user interface and helps them learn basic skills they can use in all Windows applications.

- Real-World Case — The case study used throughout the textbook is designed to be "real-world" in nature and representative of the kinds of activities that students will encounter when working with a Web browser. With a real-world case, the process of solving the problem will be more meaningful to students.

- End of Unit Material — Each unit concludes with a Task Reference that summarizes the various methods used to execute each of the skills covered in the unit. The Task Reference is followed by a meaningful Concepts Review that tests students' understanding of what they learned in the unit. The Concepts Review is followed by an Applications Review, which provides students with additional hands-on practice of the skills they learned in the unit. The Applications Review is followed by Independent Challenges, which pose open-ended, real-world case problems for students to solve. The Independent Challenges allow students to learn by exploring, and develop critical thinking skills.

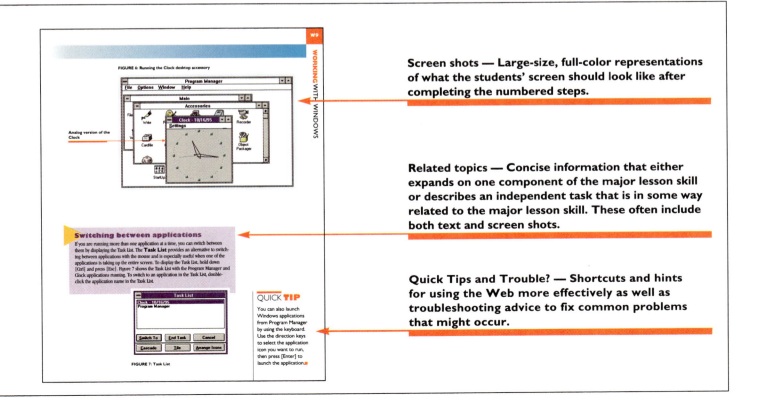

Screen shots — Large-size, full-color representations of what the students' screen should look like after completing the numbered steps.

Related topics — Concise information that either expands on one component of the major lesson skill or describes an independent task that is in some way related to the major lesson skill. These often include both text and screen shots.

Quick Tips and Trouble? — Shortcuts and hints for using the Web more effectively as well as troubleshooting advice to fix common problems that might occur.

The Student Disk

The Student Disk contains all the data files students need to complete the step-by-step lessons. For information on how to get a copy of the Student Disk, refer to the inside front or inside back cover of this book.

Adopters of this text are granted the right to post the Student Disk on any standalone computer or network used by students who have purchased this product.

For more information on the Student Disk, see the page in this book called "Read This Before You Begin The World Wide Web."

The Supplements

Complementary resources are available to you on-line. They are quality assurance tested and include:

- Lecture Notes—These are written by the authors and include pointers to other valuable Internet resources.
- Unit Summaries—An overview of the important skills and concepts students will learn in each Unit.
- Solutions—Included are solutions to all lessons, Concepts Reviews, Application Reviews, and Independent Challenges.
- Extra Problems—Included are at least two additional Independent Challenges per unit to give assignment flexibility.
- Figure Bank—A collection of all of the figures in this book in GIF format for your presentation needs.

Acknowledgments

The inspiration, perspiration, and diligence of a lot of folks went into the creation of this book. We thank our reviewers for their many valuable suggestions: Sorel Reisman, California State University at Fullerton and Angela Ambrosia, Phoenix College. Our developmental editor, Kim Crowley, deserves stellar recognition for her insightful and persistent efforts in keeping us focused on teaching valuable skills within the context of an interesting and relevant case. Thanks to Mac Mendelsohn, acquisitions editor and really nice guy, Nicole Jones Pinard, product manager and tireless cheerleader, Chris Greacen, godfather of the online companion, and the rest of the great team at Course Technology, Inc.

We would also like to thank Bob Toshack for his assistance with the figures in this book. Finally, a special acknowledgment to our daughter, Melissa, who's patience and understanding extends well beyond the realm of childhood.

Donald and Chia-Ling Barker

Brief Contents

Contents

TABLES

Read This Before You Begin
Working with Windows

To the Student

The Working with Windows section gives you practice using the main features of Windows, the control program that lets you work easily with your computer and many programs you run. You need a Student Disk to complete this section.

For information on getting a copy of the Student Disk, refer to the inside front or inside back cover of this book. See your instructor or technical support person for further information.

To the Instructor

Student Disk

Students need a copy of a Student Disk to complete the units in this book. For information on getting a copy of the Student Disk, refer to the inside front or inside back cover of this book. Your students will need the Student Disk to create a practice directory called MY_FILES.

If you choose to make the Student Disk files available to students over a network, then be sure to tell students where you want them to create the MY_FILES directory. For more information on the Student Disk, refer to the "Read This Before You Begin The World Wide Web" page.

Screens

This Working with Windows section assumes students will use the default Windows setup. If you want your students' screens to look like those in the figures, set up the Program Manager window to look like Figure 1, and make sure the Clock accessory is in analog mode with the title bar displayed at the top.

OBJECTIVES

▶ Start Windows

▶ Use the mouse

▶ Use Program
   Manager groups

▶ Run an application

▶ Resize a window

▶ Use menus and
   dialog boxes

▶ Save a file

▶ Use File Manager

▶ Arrange windows
   and icons

▶ Exit Windows

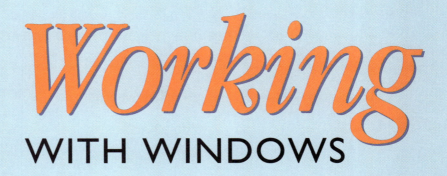

Working
WITH WINDOWS

Microsoft Windows 3.1 is the **graphical user interface** (GUI) that works hand in hand with MS-DOS to control the basic operation of your computer and the programs you run on it. Windows is a comprehensive control program that helps you run useful, task-oriented programs known as **applications**. ▶ This introduction will help you to learn basic skills that you can use in all Windows applications. First you'll learn how to start Windows and how to use the mouse in the Windows environment. Next you'll get some hands-on experience with Program Manager, and you'll learn how to work with groups, run an application, resize a window, use menus and dialog boxes, save files, use File Manager, and arrange windows and icons. Then you'll learn how to exit a Windows application and exit Windows itself. ▶

Starting Windows

Windows is started, or **launched**, from MS-DOS with the Win command. Once started, Windows takes over most of the duties of MS-DOS and provides a graphical environment in which you run your applications. Windows has several advantages over MS-DOS. As a graphical interface, it uses meaningful pictures and symbols known as **icons** to replace hard-to-remember commands. Windows lets you run more than one application at a time, so you can run, for example, a word processor and a spreadsheet at the same time and easily share data between them. ▶ Each application is represented in a rectangular space called a **window**. The Windows environment also includes several useful desktop accessories, including Clock and Notepad, which you can use for day-to-day tasks. ▶ Try starting Windows now.

1 Turn on your computer

The computer displays some technical information as it starts up and tests its circuitry. MS-DOS starts automatically, then displays the **command prompt** (usually C:\>). The command prompt gives you access to MS-DOS commands and applications. If your computer is set up so that it automatically runs Windows when it starts, the command prompt will not display. You can then skip Step 2.

2 Type win then press [Enter]

This command starts Windows. The screen momentarily goes blank while the computer starts Windows. An hourglass displays, indicating Windows is busy processing a command. Then the Windows Program Manager displays on your screen, as shown in Figure 1. Your screen might look slightly different depending on which applications are installed on your computer.

TABLE 1:
Elements of the Windows desktop

DESKTOP ELEMENT	DESCRIPTION
Program Manager	The main control program of Windows. All Windows applications are started from the Program Manager.
Window	A rectangular space framed by a double border on the screen. The Program Manager is framed in a window.
Application icon	The graphic representation of a Windows application.
Title bar	The area directly below the window's top border that displays the name of a window or application.
Sizing buttons	Buttons in the upper-right corner of a window that you can use to minimize or maximize a window.
Menu bar	The area under the title bar on a window. The menu bar provides access to most of an application's commands.
Control menu box	A box in the upper-left corner of each window; provides a menu used to resize, move, maximize, minimize, or close a window. Double-clicking this box closes a window or an application.
Mouse pointer	An arrow indicating the current location of the mouse on the desktop.

FIGURE 1: Program Manager window

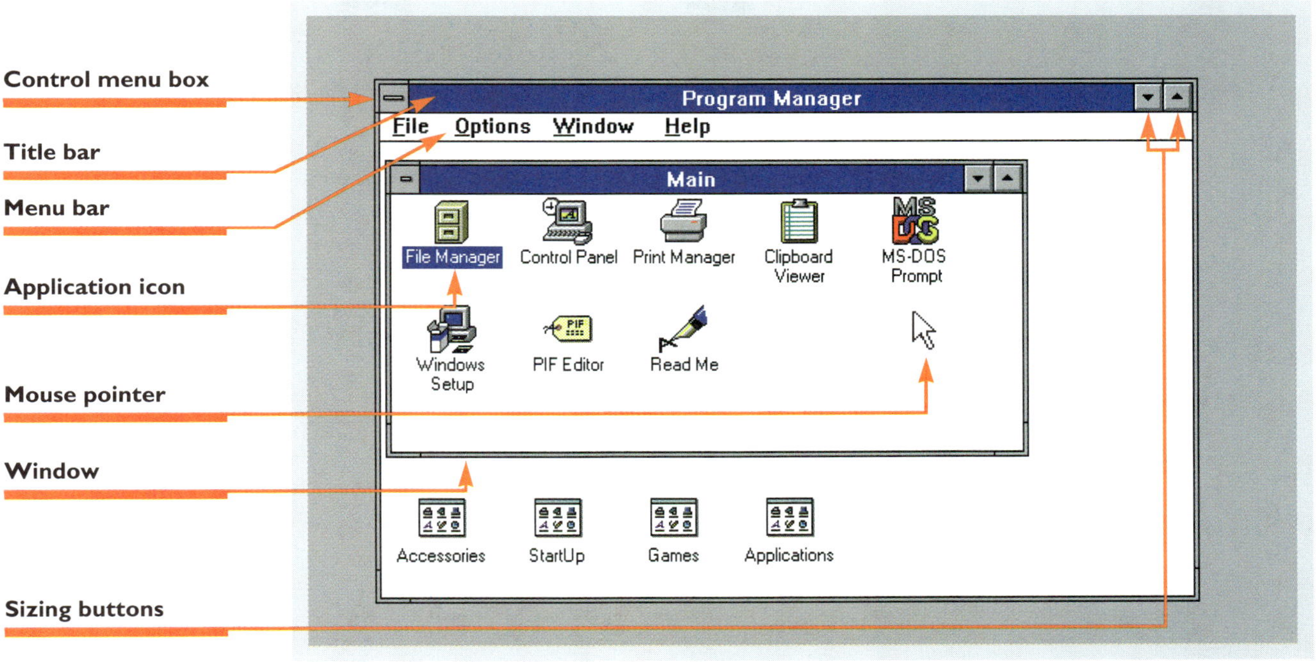

Control menu box

Title bar

Menu bar

Application icon

Mouse pointer

Window

Sizing buttons

[Program Manager window showing: Program Manager title bar with File, Options, Window, Help menu bar; Main window containing File Manager, Control Panel, Print Manager, Clipboard Viewer, MS-DOS Prompt, Windows Setup, PIF Editor, Read Me icons; and Accessories, StartUp, Games, Applications group icons.]

The Windows desktop

The entire screen area on the monitor represents the Windows desktop. The **desktop** is an electronic version of a desk that provides workspace for different computing tasks. Windows allows you to customize the desktop to support the way you like to work and to organize the applications you need to run. Use Table 1 to identify the key elements of the desktop, referring to Figure 1 for their locations. Because the Windows desktop can be customized, your desktop might look slightly different.

Using the mouse

The **mouse** is a handheld input device that you roll on your desk to position the mouse pointer on the Windows desktop. When you move the mouse on your desk, the **mouse pointer** on the screen moves in the same direction. The buttons on the mouse are used to select icons and choose commands, and to indicate the work to be done in applications. Table 2 lists the four basic mouse techniques. Table 3 shows some common mouse pointer shapes. ▶ Try using the mouse now.

1 Locate the mouse pointer ⍩ on the Windows desktop and move the mouse across your desk

Watch how the mouse pointer moves on the Windows desktop in response to your movements. Try moving the mouse pointer in circles, then back and forth in straight lines.

2 Position the mouse pointer over the Control Panel icon in the Main group window

Positioning the mouse pointer over an icon is called **pointing**. The Control Panel icon is a graphical representation of the Control Panel application, a special program that controls the operation of the Windows environment. If the Control Panel icon is not visible in the Main group window, point to any other icon. The Program Manager is customizable so the Control Panel could be hidden from view.

3 Press and release the left mouse button

Pressing and releasing the mouse button is called **clicking**. When you position the mouse pointer on an icon in Program Manager then click, you **select** the icon. When the Control Panel icon is selected, its title is highlighted, as shown in Figure 2. If you clicked an icon that caused a menu to open, click the icon again to close the menu. You'll learn about menus later. Now practice a mouse skill called **dragging**.

4 With the icon selected, press and hold the left mouse button and move the mouse down and to the right

The icon moves with the mouse pointer, as shown in Figure 3. When you release the mouse button, the icon relocates in the group window.

5 Drag the Control Panel icon back to its original position

TABLE 2:
Basic mouse techniques

TECHNIQUE	HOW TO DO IT
Pointing	Move the mouse pointer to position it over an item on the desktop.
Clicking	Press and release the mouse button.
Double-clicking	Press and release the mouse button twice quickly.
Dragging	Point at an item, press and hold the mouse button, move the mouse to a new location, then release the mouse button.

FIGURE 2: Selecting an icon

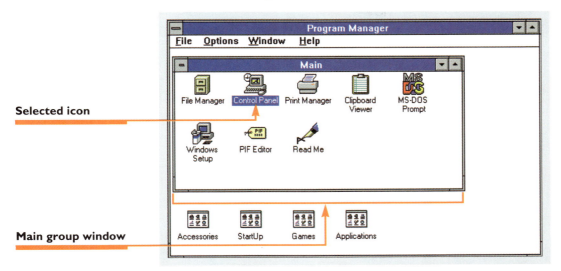

Selected icon

Main group window

FIGURE 3: Dragging an icon

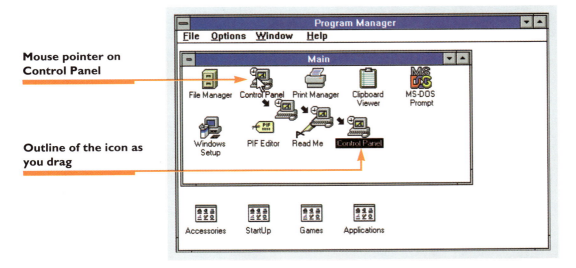

Mouse pointer on
Control Panel

Outline of the icon as
you drag

TABLE 3: Common mouse pointer shapes

SHAPE	USED TO
⬦	Select items, choose commands, start applications, and work in applications.
I	Position mouse pointer for editing or inserting text. This icon is called an insertion point.
⧖	Indicate Windows is busy processing a command.
⟷	Change the size of a window. This icon appears when mouse pointer is on the border of a window.

Using Program Manager groups

In Program Manager, you launch applications and organize your applications into windows called groups. A **group** can appear as an open window or as an icon in the Program Manager window. Each group has a name related to its contents, and you can reorganize the groups to suit your needs. The standard Windows groups are described in Table 4. ▶ Try working with groups now.

1 If necessary, double-click the **Main group icon** to open the Main group window

The Main group icon is usually located at the bottom of the Program Manager window.

2 Double-click the **Accessories group icon**

When you double-click the Accessories group icon, it expands into the Accessories group window, as shown in Figure 4. Now move the Accessories group window to the right.

3 Click the **Accessories group window title bar** and drag the group window to the right

An outline of the window moves to the right with the mouse. When you release the mouse button, the Accessories group window moves to the location you've indicated. Moving a window lets you see what is beneath it. Any window in the Windows environment can be moved with this technique.

4 Click the **title bar** of the Main group window

The Main group window becomes the **active window**, the one you are currently working in. Other windows, including the Accessories group window, are considered background windows. Note that the active window has a highlighted title bar. Program Manager has a highlighted title bar because it is the **active application**.

5 Activate the **Accessories group window** by clicking anywhere in that window

The Accessories group window moves to the foreground again. Now try closing the Accessories group window to an icon.

6 Double-click the **control menu box** in the Accessories group window

When you double-click this box, the Accessories group window shrinks to an icon and the Main group window becomes the active window. Double-clicking the control menu box is the easiest way to close a window or an application.

TABLE 4:
Standard Windows groups

GROUP NAME	CONTENTS
Main	Applications that control how Windows works; the primary Windows group.
Accessories	Useful desktop accessories for day-to-day tasks.
StartUp	Programs that run automatically when Windows is started.
Games	Game programs for Windows.
Applications	Group of applications found on your hard disk.

FIGURE 4: Accessories group expanded into a window

Main group window title bar

Control menu box

Highlighted title bar indicates active window

Accessories group window

Program Manager group icons

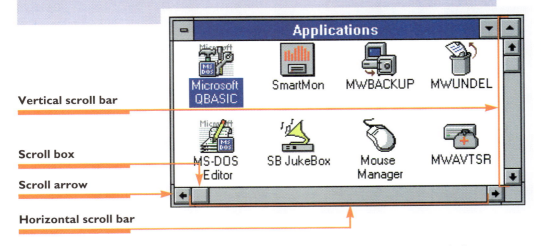

Scroll bars

If a group contains more icons than can be displayed at one time, **scroll bars** appear on the right and/or bottom edges of the window to give you access to the remaining icons, as shown in Figure 5. Vertical or horizontal arrows appear at the ends of the bars. To use scroll bars, click the vertical or horizontal arrows that point in the direction you want the window to scroll or drag the scroll box along the scroll bar. Scroll bars appear whenever there is more information than can fit in a window. You'll see them in many Windows applications.

Vertical scroll bar

Scroll box

Scroll arrow

Horizontal scroll bar

FIGURE 5: Vertical and horizontal scroll bars on a window

QUICK **TIP**

You can use the direction keys on the keyboard to scroll the contents of the active window. To scroll vertically, press [↑] or [↓]. To scroll horizontally, press [←] or [→].■

Running an application

A Windows application is a program specially designed to operate, or **run**, in the Windows environment. Windows comes with several built-in Windows applications, including the desktop accessories shown in Table 5. Windows applications are represented by graphical icons in Program Manager groups. To run a Windows application, double-click the application icon. ▶ Try running the Clock application now.

1 Double-click the **Accessories group icon**

The Accessories group window opens and the desktop accessory icons display inside it. You may need to move the Main window to see the Accessories group icon.

2 Double-click the **Clock application icon**

The Clock application starts and Windows displays an analog clock in a window, as shown in Figure 6. You might see a digital clock, depending on your system settings. Note that the current date appears on the clock's title bar and the current time appears on the clock's face. The Clock application is running, as demonstrated by the moving second hand.

3 Click the **Clock title bar** then drag the window to the lower-right corner of the screen

If the clock does not have a title bar, double-click the clock to display the title bar. The clock continues running in the lower-right corner of the screen. The Clock application window is like any other window and can be moved anywhere on the desktop. Sometimes it's useful to change the location of an application on the desktop so you can see information contained in other windows.

4 Close the Clock by double-clicking the **Clock window control menu box**

The Clock application closes and is no longer visible on the screen. Double-clicking an application's control menu box closes the application and returns you to the application's group window.

TABLE 5: Some common Windows applications in the Accessories group

APPLICATION	PURPOSE
Write	Word processor
Paintbrush	Drawing program
Notepad	Simple editor/note taker
Cardfile	Card file program
Calendar	Electronic calendar/appointment planner
Calculator	Calculator
Clock	Digital/analog clock

FIGURE 6: Running the Clock desktop accessory

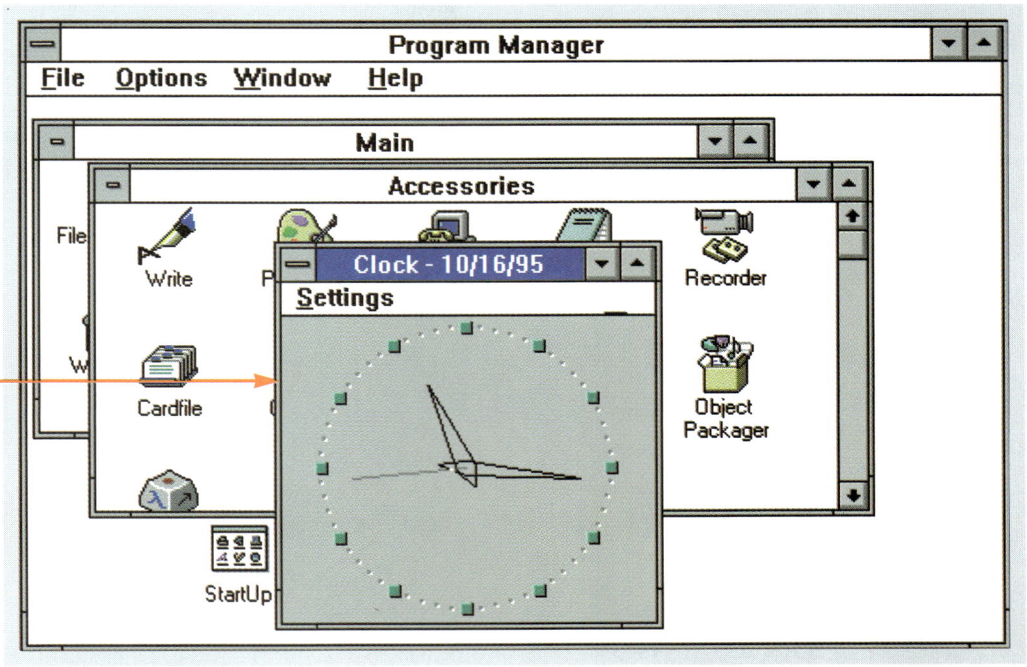

Analog version of the Clock →

Switching between applications

If you are running more than one application at a time, you can switch between them by displaying the Task List. The **Task List** provides an alternative to switching between applications with the mouse and is especially useful when one of the applications is taking up the entire screen. To display the Task List, hold down [Ctrl] and press [Esc]. Figure 7 shows the Task List with the Program Manager and Clock applications running. To switch to an application in the Task List, double-click the application name in the Task List.

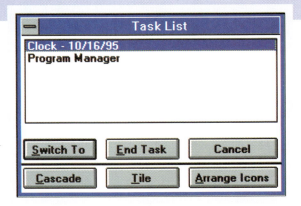

FIGURE 7: Task List

Resizing a window

The Windows desktop can get cluttered with icons and windows if you use lots of applications. Each window is surrounded by a standard border and sizing buttons that allow you to minimize, maximize, and restore windows as needed. The sizing buttons are shown in Table 6. They help you keep the desktop organized. ▶ Try sizing the Clock window now.

1 Double-click the **Clock application icon**
The Clock application restarts.

2 Click the **Minimize button** in the upper-right corner of the Clock window
The Minimize button is the sizing button on the left. When you **minimize** the clock, it shrinks to an icon at the bottom of the screen, as shown in Figure 8. Notice that the Clock icon continues to show the right time, even as an icon. Windows applications continue to run after you minimize them.

3 Double-click the **Clock icon** to restore the Clock window to its original size
The clock is restored to its original size, and the application continues to run.

4 Click the **Maximize button** in the upper-right corner of the Clock window
The Maximize button is the sizing button to the right of the Minimize button. When you **maximize** the clock, it takes up the entire screen, as shown in Figure 9. Although it's unlikely you'll want to maximize this application very often, you'll find the ability to maximize other Windows applications very useful.

5 Click the **Restore button** in the upper-right corner of the Clock window
The Restore button, as shown in Figure 9, is located to the right of the Minimize button *after* an application has been maximized. The Restore button returns an application to its original size.

6 Double-click the **Clock window control menu box** to close the application

TABLE 6:
Buttons for managing windows

BUTTON	PURPOSE
▼	Minimizes an application to an icon on the bottom of the screen.
▲	Maximizes an application to its largest possible size.
⬍	Restores an application, returning it to its original size.

FIGURE 8:
Minimized Clock application as an icon

Minimize button

Maximize button

Minimized clock with current time and date

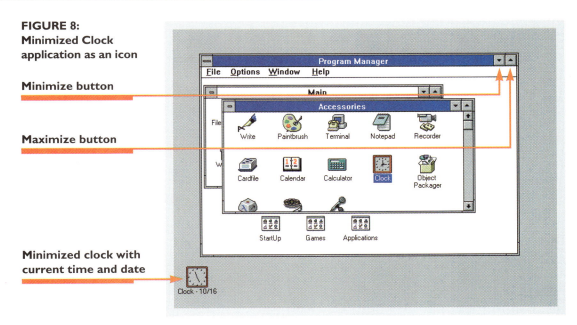

FIGURE 9:
Maximized clock filling entire screen

Restore button appears after a window has been maximized

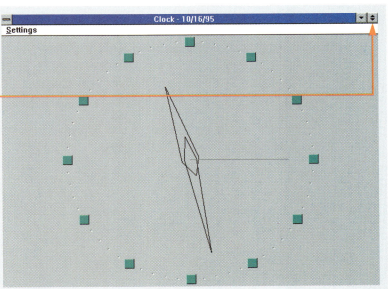

Changing the dimension of a window

The dimension of a window can also be changed, but the window will always be a rectangle. To change the dimension of a window, position the mouse pointer on the window border you want to modify. The mouse pointer changes to ⟨⟶⟩. Drag the border in the direction you want to change. Figure 10 shows the width of the Clock window being increased, which will make the clock face larger.

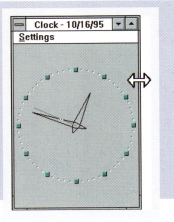

FIGURE 10: Increasing the width of the Clock window

Using menus and dialog boxes

A **menu** is a list of commands that you can use to accomplish certain tasks. Each Windows application has its own set of menus, which are listed on the **menu bar** along the top of the application window. Sometimes when you select a command from a menu, the application needs more information before it can complete the task, in which case a **dialog box** opens, giving you more options. See Table 7 for some of the typical conventions used on menus and dialog boxes. ▶ Try using the Control Panel which lets you customize your Windows desktop.

STEPS

1   Click the **Main group window** to make it active, then double-click the **Control Panel icon**

Drag other windows out of the way, if necessary. The Control Panel window opens.

2   Click **Settings** on the menu bar

A menu displays listing all the commands that let you adjust different aspects of your desktop. See Table 7.

3   Click **Desktop** to display the Desktop dialog box

This dialog box provides options to customize your desktop. See Figure 11. Next, locate the Screen Saver section of the dialog box. A **screen saver** is a moving pattern that fills your screen after your computer has not been used for a specified amount of time.

4   Click the **Name list arrow** in the Screen Saver section

A list of available screen saver patterns displays.

5   Click the screen saver pattern of your choice, then click **Test**

The Test button is a **command button**. The two most common command buttons are OK and Cancel which you'll see in almost every dialog box. The screen saver pattern you chose displays. It will remain on the screen until you move the mouse or press a key.

6   Move the mouse to exit the screen saver

Next, you'll adjust the cursor blink rate in the Cursor Blink Rate section. The **cursor** is the vertical line that shows you where you are on the screen. See Figure 11.

7   Drag the scroll box all the way to the right of the scroll bar, then click the **left arrow** in the scroll bar a few times

By moving the scroll box between Slow and Fast on the scroll bar, you can adjust the cursor blink rate to suit your needs.

8   Click **OK** to save your changes and close the dialog box

Clicking OK accepts your changes; clicking Cancel rejects your changes. Now you can exit the Control Panel.

9   Double-click the **Control Panel control menu box** to close this window

FIGURE 11:
Desktop dialog box

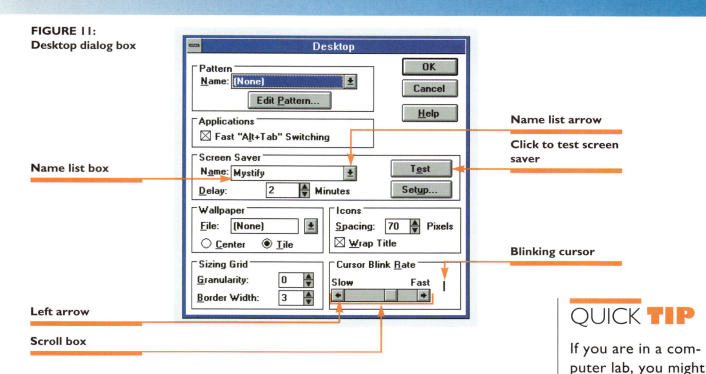

Name list arrow

Click to test screen saver

Name list box

Left arrow

Scroll box

Blinking cursor

QUICK **TIP**

If you are in a computer lab, you might want to return the desktop settings you changed to their original state.■

TABLE 7: Typical items on menus and dialog boxes

ITEM	MEANING	EXAMPLE
Dimmed command	A menu command that is not currently available.	Undo
Ellipsis	Choosing this menu command opens a dialog box that asks for further information.	Paste Special...
Triangle	Clicking this button opens a cascading menu containing an additional list of menu commands.	Axis ▶
Keyboard shortcut	A keyboard alternative for executing a menu command.	Cut Ctrl+X
Underlined letter	Pressing the underlined letter executes this menu command.	Copy Right
Check box	Clicking this square box turns a dialog box option on or off.	☒ Wrap Title
Text box	A box in which you type text.	tours.wk4
Radio button	Clicking this small circle selects a single dialog box option.	◉ Tile
Command button	Clicking this button executes this dialog box command.	OK
List box	A box containing a list of items. To choose an item, click the list arrow, then click the desired item.	c: ms-dos_5

Saving a file

The documents you create using a computer are stored in the computer's random access memory (RAM). **RAM** is temporary storage space that is erased when the computer is turned off. To store a document permanently, you need to save it to a disk. You can either save your work to a 3.5-inch or a 5.25-inch disk that you insert into the disk drive of your computer (i.e., drive A or B), or a hard disk, which is a disk built into the computer (usually drive C). Your instructor has provided you with a Student Disk to use as you proceed through the lessons in this book. This book assumes that you will save all of your files to your Student Disk. Refer to the Read This Before You Begin page immediately preceding this section for more information on your Student Disk. ▶ In this lesson, you'll create a simple document using Notepad, then you will save the document to your Student Disk. **Notepad** is a simple text editor that lets you create memos, record notes, or edit text files. A **text file** is a document containing words, letters, or numbers, but no special computer instructions, such as formatting.

1 Insert your Student Disk into drive A or drive B
Check with your instructor if you aren't sure which drive you should use.

2 Click the **Accessories group window** to activate it

3 Double-click the **Notepad application icon** to start Notepad
The Notepad application starts, and the Notepad window displays. Now, enter some text.

4 Type **Today I started working with Notepad.** then press **[Enter]**
Your screen should look like Figure 12.

5 Click **File** on the Notepad menu bar, then click **Save**
The Save As dialog box displays, as shown in Figure 13. In this dialog box you enter a name for your file and specify where you want to save it.

6 Type **MYNOTES** in the File Name text box
Your entry replaces the highlighted (selected) *.txt. Notepad will automatically add the extension when you click OK. Now you need to specify the drive where your Student Disk is located.

7 Click the **Drives list arrow** to display the drives on your computer, then click **a:** or **b:**, depending on which drive contains your Student Disk
Notice that the list of files that are on your Student Disk displays below the File Name text box.

8 Click **OK**
The Save As dialog box closes and MYNOTES is now saved on your Student Disk.

9 Click **File** on the Notepad menu bar, then click **Exit** to close Notepad

FIGURE 12: Notepad window with text entered

Menu bar

Cursor

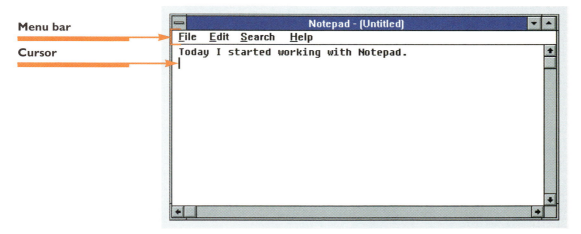

FIGURE 13: Save As dialog box

Highlighted File Name
text box

Your list of directories
might be different

Drives list arrow

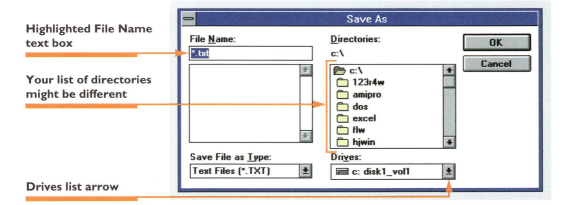

QUICK **TIP**

Save your work
often, at least every
15 minutes and
before printing.■

Using File Manager

File Manager is an application included with Windows that can help you organize files and directories. A **directory** is like a file folder—it is a part of a disk where you can store a group of related files. For example, you might want to create a directory called PROJECT1 and store all of the files relating to a particular project in that directory. You can use File Manager to create the directory, then move the related files into it.

▶ Use File Manager to create a directory called MY_FILES on your Student Disk and then move the Notepad file you created and saved in the previous lesson into that directory. Make sure your Student Disk is in drive A or drive B before beginning the steps.

1 Double-click the **Main program group icon**, or if it is already open, click the **Main group window** to activate it

2 Double-click the **File Manager application icon** in the Main group window
   File Manager opens to display the directory window, as shown in Figure 14. Your File Manager will contain different files and directories. The directory window is divided by the split bar. The left side of the window displays the structure of the current drive, or the directory tree. The right side of the window displays a list of files in the selected directory. See Table 8 for a description of the various icons used in the directory window. The status bar displays the information about the current drive and directory and other information to help you with file management tasks.

3 Click the **drive icon** that corresponds to the drive containing your Student Disk
   The contents of your Student Disk displays. Now create a directory on this disk.

4 Click **File** on the menu bar, then click **Create Directory**
   The Create Directory dialog box displays listing the current directory, which in this case is the top level directory indicated by the backslash (\). You will type a new directory name in the text box provided. Directory names can have up to 11 characters but cannot include spaces, commas, or backslashes.

5 Type **MY_FILES** in the Name text box, then click **OK**
   You can type in the directory name in either uppercase or lowercase letters. The new directory appears in both sides of the directory window.

6 Press and hold the mouse button to select MYNOTES.TXT, then drag the file into the MY_FILES directory on the left side of the window
   The mouse pointer changes as you drag the file, as shown in Figure 15. Don't worry if you move a file to the wrong place; simply drag it again to the correct location. (You can drag it to the MY_FILES directory in either the left or right side of the window.)

7 Click **Yes** in the Confirm Mouse Operation dialog box
   Notice that the file no longer appears in the list of files. Now check that the file is in the newly created directory.

8 Double-click the **MY_FILES icon**
   The file appears in the list of files. If you want, you can use this directory throughout this book to store the files that you save. Now that you have created a directory and moved a file into it, you can exit File Manager.

9 Double-click the **control menu box** to exit File Manager

FIGURE 14: File Manager

Menu bar

Drive icons

Directory tree

Selected directory

Status bar

Split bar

List of files

Directory window

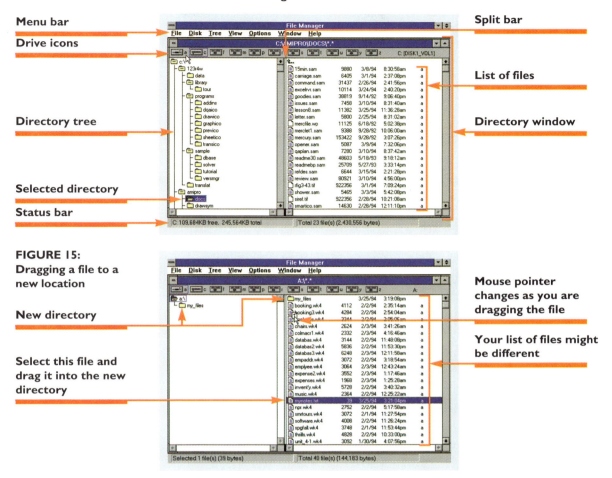

FIGURE 15:
Dragging a file to a new location

New directory

Select this file and drag it into the new directory

Mouse pointer changes as you are dragging the file

Your list of files might be different

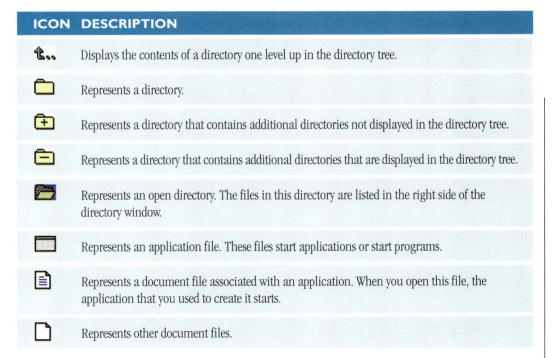

TABLE 8: Directory window icons

ICON	DESCRIPTION
	Displays the contents of a directory one level up in the directory tree.
	Represents a directory.
	Represents a directory that contains additional directories not displayed in the directory tree.
	Represents a directory that contains additional directories that are displayed in the directory tree.
	Represents an open directory. The files in this directory are listed in the right side of the directory window.
	Represents an application file. These files start applications or start programs.
	Represents a document file associated with an application. When you open this file, the application that you used to create it starts.
	Represents other document files.

QUICK **TIP**

To select a group of files, click the first file, then press [Shift] and click the last file. To select noncontiguous files (files not next to each other in the file list), click the first file, then press [Ctrl] and click each additional file.

Arranging windows and icons

If your desktop contains many groups that you open regularly, you might find that the open windows clutter your desktop. The Tile and Cascade commands on the Window menu let you view all your open group windows at once in an organized arrangement. You can also use the Window menu to open all the program groups installed on your computer. ▶ Once you are comfortable working with Windows, you might decide to reorganize your group windows. You can easily move an icon from one group window to another by dragging it with the mouse. In the following steps, you'll drag the Clock icon from the Accessories group window to the StartUp group window. The StartUp group window contains programs that automatically start running when you launch Windows.

1 Click the **Program Manager Maximize button** to maximize this window, then click **Window** on the menu bar

The Window menu opens, as shown in Figure 16, displaying the commands Cascade, Tile, and Arrange Icons, followed by a numbered list of the program groups installed on your computer. You might see a check mark next to one of the items, indicating that this program group is the active one. Locate StartUp on the numbered list. If you don't see StartUp, click More Windows at the bottom of the list, then double-click StartUp in the dialog box that displays. If you still can't find StartUp, see your instructor or technical support person for assistance.

2 Click **StartUp**

The StartUp group window opens. Depending on how your computer is set up, you might see some program icons already in this window. At this point, your screen is getting cluttered with three program group windows open (Main, Accessories, and StartUp). Use the Cascade command to arrange them in an orderly way.

3 Click **Window** on the menu bar, then click **Cascade**

The windows display in a layered arrangement, with the title bars of each showing. This formation is neatly organized and shows all your open group windows, but it doesn't allow you to easily drag the Clock icon from the Accessories group window to the StartUp group window. The Tile command arranges the windows so that the contents of all the open windows are visible.

4 Click **Window** on the menu bar, then click **Tile**

The windows are now positioned in an ideal way to copy an icon from one window to another. Before continuing to step 5, locate the Clock icon in the Accessories group window. If you don't see the icon, use the scroll bar to bring it into view.

5 Drag the Clock application icon from the Accessories group window to the StartUp group window

Your screen now looks like Figure 17. The Clock application will automatically start the next time Windows is launched. If you are working on your own computer and want to leave the Clock in the StartUp group, skip Step 6 and continue to the next lesson, "Exiting Windows." If you are working in a computer lab, move the Clock icon back to its original location in the Accessories group window.

6 Drag the Clock application icon from the StartUp group window to the Accessories group window

The Clock icon is now back in the Accessories group.

FIGURE 16:
Window menu

Check mark indicates the active program group

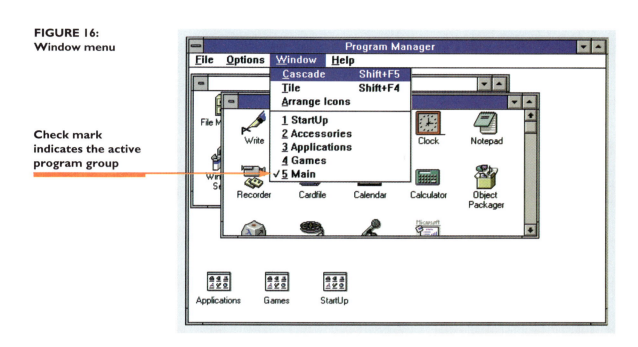

FIGURE 17:
Tiled group windows

StartUp group window with Clock icon

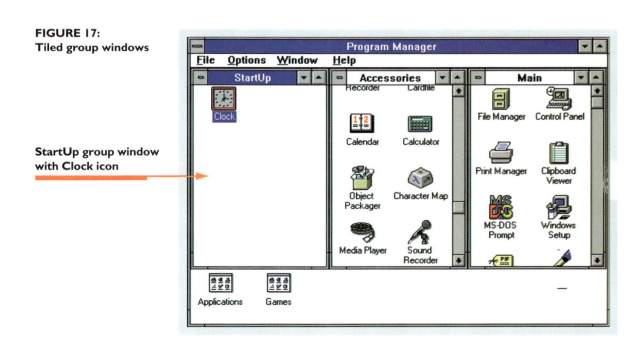

QUICK **TIP**

To move a copy of an icon from one group window to another, hold down [Ctrl] as you drag the icon.

Exiting Windows

When you are finished working with Windows, close all the applications you are running and exit Windows. Do not turn off the computer while Windows is running; you could lose important data if you turn off your computer too soon. ▶ Now try closing all your active applications and exiting Windows.

1 Close any active applications or group windows by double-clicking the control menu boxes of the open windows, one at a time

The windows close. If you have any unsaved changes in your application, a dialog box displays, asking if you want to save them.

2 Click **File** on the Program Manager menu bar

The File menu displays, as shown in Figure 18.

3 Click **Exit Windows**

Program Manager displays the Exit Windows dialog box, as shown in Figure 19. You have two options at this point: Click OK to exit Windows, or click Cancel to abort the Exit Windows command and return to the Program Manager.

4 Click **OK** to exit Windows

Windows finishes its work and the MS-DOS command prompt appears. You can now safely turn off the computer.

FIGURE 18: Exiting Windows using the File menu

Menu bar

Exit Windows command

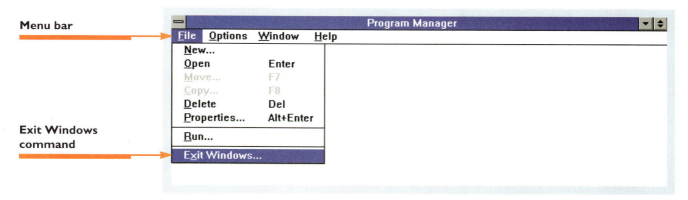

FIGURE 19: Exit Windows dialog box

Exiting Windows with the Program Manager control menu box

You can also exit Windows by double-clicking the control menu box in the upper-left corner of the Program Manager window, as shown in Figure 20. After you double-click the control menu box, you see the Exit Windows dialog box. Click OK to exit Windows.

Double-click the control menu box

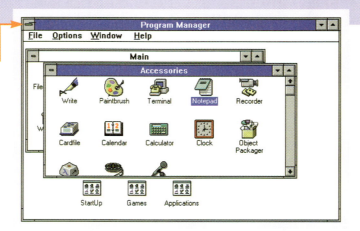

FIGURE 20: Exiting Windows with the Program Manager control menu box

TROUBLE?

If you do not exit from Windows before turning off the computer, you might lose data from the applications you used while you were running Windows. Always close your applications and exit from Windows before turning off your computer. Do not turn off the computer if you are in a computer lab.■

CONCEPTSREVIEW

**Label each of the elements
of the Windows screen
shown in Figure 21.**

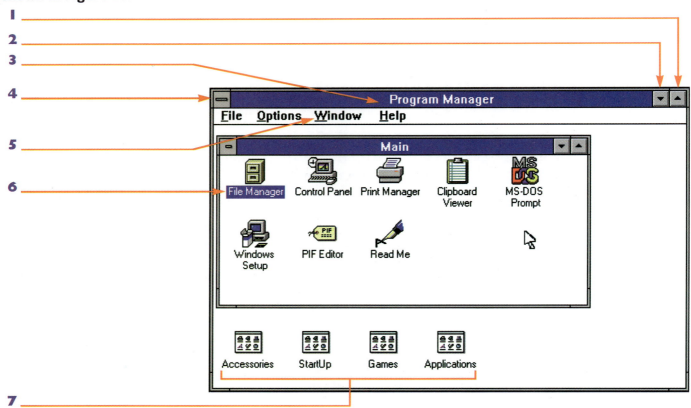

FIGURE 21

**Match each of the statements with the term
it describes.**

8 Shrinks an application
window to an icon

9 Displays the name of the
window or application

10 Serves as a launching pad
for all applications

11 Requests more information
that you supply before execut-
ing command

12 Lets the user point at screen
menus and icons

a. Program Manager

b. Dialog box

c. Mouse

d. Title bar

e. Minimize button

Select the best answer from the list of choices.

13 The acronym GUI means:

a. Grayed user information

b. Group user icons

c. Graphical user interface

d. Group user interconnect

14 The term for starting Windows is:

a. Prompting

b. Launching

c. Applying

d. Processing

15 The small pictures that represent items such as applications are:

a. Icons

b. Windows

c. Buttons

d. Pointers

16 All of the following are examples of using a mouse, EXCEPT:

a. Clicking the Maximize button

b. Pressing [Enter]

c. Pointing at the control menu box

d. Dragging the Games icon

17 When Windows is busy performing a task, the mouse pointer changes to a(n):

a. Hand

b. Arrow

c Clock

d. Hourglass

18 The term for moving an item to a new location on the desktop is:

a. Pointing

b. Clicking

c. Dragging

d. Restoring

19 The Clock, Notepad, and Calendar applications in Windows are known as:

a. Menu commands

b. Control panels

c. Sizing buttons

d. Desktop accessories

20 The Maximize button is used to:

a. Return a window to its original size

b. Expand a window to fill the computer screen

c. Scroll slowly through a window

d. Run programs from the main menu

21 What appears if a window contains more information than can be displayed in the window?

a. Program icon

b. Cascading menu

c. Scroll bars

d. Check box

22 A window is active when its title bar is:

a. Highlighted

b. Dimmed

c. Checked

d. Underlined

23 What is the term for changing the dimensions of a window?

a. Selecting

b. Resizing

c. Navigating

d. Scrolling

24 The menu bar provides access to an application's functions through:

a. Icons

b. Scroll bars

c. Commands

d. Control menu box

25 File Manager is a Windows application that lets you:

a. Select a different desktop wallpaper

b. Move a file from one location to another

c. Type entries into a text file

d. Determine what programs begin automatically when you start Windows

26 When your desktop is too cluttered, you can organize it by all the following methods, EXCEPT:

a. Double-clicking the control menu box to close unneeded windows

b. Using the Tile command to view all open group windows

c. Using the Cascade command to open group window title bars

d. Clicking File, clicking Exit Windows, then clicking OK

27 You can exit Windows by double-clicking the:

a. Accessories group icon

b. Program Manager control menu box

c. Main window menu bar

d. Control Panel application

APPLICATIONS
REVIEW

1 Start Windows and identify items on the screen.

  a. Turn on the computer, if necessary.

  b. At the command prompt, type "WIN," then press [Enter]. After Windows loads, the Program Manager displays.

  c. Try to identify as many items on the desktop as you can, without referring to the lesson material. Then compare your results with Figure 1.

2 Minimize and restore the Program Manager window.

  a. Click the Minimize button. Notice that the Program Manager window reduces to an icon at the bottom of the screen. Now try restoring the window.

  b. Double-click the minimized Program Manager icon. The Program Manager window opens.

  c. Practice minimizing and restoring other windows on the desktop.

3 Resize and move the Program Manager window.

  a. Click anywhere inside the Program Manager window to activate the window.

  b. Move the mouse pointer over the lower-right corner of the Program Manager window. Notice that the mouse pointer changes to a double-ended arrow.

  c. Press and hold the mouse button and drag the corner of the window up and to the right until the Program Manager takes up the top third of your screen.

  d. Drag the Program Manager title bar to reposition the window at the bottom of the screen.

4 Practice working with menus and dialog boxes.

  a. Click Window on the Program Manager menu bar, then click Accessories (if you can't find it in the menu, click More Windows, then double-click it from the list that appears, scrolling if necessary).

  b. Double-click the Calculator icon to open the Calculator application.

  c. Click numbers and operators as you would on a handheld calculator to perform some simple arithmetic operations, like 22 multiplied by 3.99, to see how much it would cost to take a bus of 22 employees on the way back from a conference to a fast-food place for a quick lunch. (Multiplication is indicated by an asterisk *.)

  d. Double-click the Calculator control menu box when you are finished.

5 Practice working with files:

  a. Open File Manager from the Main group window.

  b. Be sure your Student Disk is in drive A or drive B, then double-click the drive icon containing your Student Disk.

  c. Double-click the drive C icon, then choose Tile from the Window menu. The open drive windows display, one above the other. If you have more windows open, double-click their control menu boxes to close them, then choose Tile again.

  d. Double-click the c:\ folder icon on the left side of the drive C window, then scroll down the left side of the drive C window using the vertical scroll bar to see the available directories. When you see the Windows folder icon, double-click it to see the directories and files available in the Windows folder.

  e. Scroll down the right side of the drive C window using the vertical scroll bar to see the files contained in the Windows folder. If you needed to copy a file from the Windows folder to your Student Disk, you could drag it from the list of files in the drive C window to the drive A window, but don't do so now.

6 Exit Windows.

  a. Close any open application by double-clicking the application's control menu box.

  b. Double-click the control menu box in the upper-left corner of the Program Manager window. The Exit Windows dialog box displays.

  c. Click OK. Windows closes and the DOS command prompt displays.

INDEPENDENT
CHALLENGE

Windows 3.1 provides an on-line tutorial which can help you master essential Windows controls and concepts. The tutorial features interactive lessons that teach you how to use Windows elements such as the mouse, Program Manager, menus, and icons. The tutorial also covers how to use Help.

The tutorial material you should use depends on your level of experience with Windows. Some users might want to review the basics of the Windows work area. Others might want to explore additional Windows topics, such as managing files and customizing windows.

Ask your instructor or technical support person about how to use the Windows tutorial.

The World Wide Web

Read This Before You Begin
The World Wide Web

To the Student

The lessons and exercises in this book feature several sites on the World Wide Web that are available on a continually updated Online Companion. To complete the step-by-step lessons, Applications Reviews, and Independent Challenges in this book, you will need access to the *World Wide Web — Illustrated* Online Companion. A link to the Online Companion is located on the *World Wide Web — Illustrated* Home Page. A link to the Student Center is also located on the *World Wide Web — Illustrated* Home Page. There, you will find chapter overviews, extra problems, a graphical glossary, and pointers to other valuable Internet resources.

In addition to the Online Companion, you must have a Student Disk. For information on getting a copy of the Student Disk, refer to the inside front or inside back cover of this book. See your instructor or technical support person for further information.

Using Your Own Computer

If you are going to work through this book using your own computer, you need a computer system running Microsoft Windows 3.1 or later, Netscape Navigator 1.1 or a comparable browser, an electronic copy of the *World Wide Web — Illustrated* Home Page, a connection to the Internet, and a Student Disk. You will not be able to complete the step-by-step lessons and exercises in this book using your own computer until you have your own copy of the *World Wide Web — Illustrated* Home Page or the URL address, file:///cl/netscape/initial.htm, and Student Disk. This book assumes the default settings under a standard installation of Netscape Navigator 1.1 except that we replace Netscape's Home Page with the *World Wide Web — Illustrated* Home Page. See your instructor for a copy of the Netscape disks if you do not have the *World Wide Web — Illustrated* Home Page.

To the Instructor

The Student Disk contains the files students need to complete the step-by-step lessons in the units, Applications Reviews, and Independent Challenges. For information on getting a copy of the Student Disk, refer to the inside front or inside back cover of this book. If you have already installed your own version of Netscape Navigator 1.1, you will need to change the default home page to the *World Wide Web — Illustrated* Home Page (i.e., the INITIAL.HTM file included on the Netscape disks). As an adopter of this text, you are granted the right to distribute the files on the Student Disk to any student who has purchased a copy of this text. You are free to post all these files to a network or standalone workstations, or simply provide copies of the Student Disk to your students. The instructions in this book assume the students know which drive and directory contain the Student Disk, so it's important that you provide disk location information before the students start working through the Units.

UNIT 1

Getting Started

WITH THE WORLD WIDE WEB

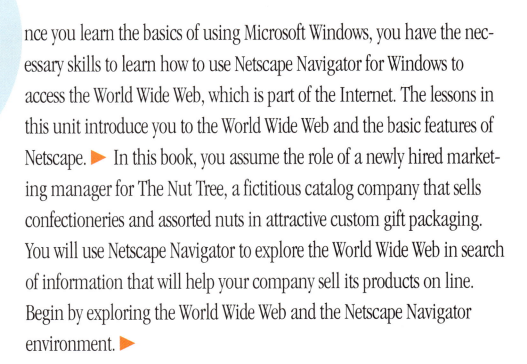

Once you learn the basics of using Microsoft Windows, you have the necessary skills to learn how to use Netscape Navigator for Windows to access the World Wide Web, which is part of the Internet. The lessons in this unit introduce you to the World Wide Web and the basic features of Netscape. ▶ In this book, you assume the role of a newly hired marketing manager for The Nut Tree, a fictitious catalog company that sells confectioneries and assorted nuts in attractive custom gift packaging. You will use Netscape Navigator to explore the World Wide Web in search of information that will help your company sell its products on line. Begin by exploring the World Wide Web and the Netscape Navigator environment. ▶

Defining Web browsers

The **Internet** is a collection of networks that connect computers all over the world. A **network** consists of two or more computers that are connected to share data. The Internet connects millions of computers using a combination of phone lines, coax cables, fiber-optic cables, satellites, and other telecommunications media, as depicted in Figure 1-1. These computers share vast amounts of information ranging from simple text to complex sound and video images. This enormous information source is available to anyone with a computer and a link to the Internet. See the related topic "Internet and World Wide Web history" to learn more about how this enormous network got started. ▶ The **World Wide Web** (also known as the Web, WWW, and W3) is a vast series of electronic documents called **Web pages** or **Web documents** that are linked together over the Internet. Web pages typically incorporate both text and graphics, as shown in Figure 1-2; however, they may include sound and video clips too. ▶ **Web browsers** are computer programs that enable you to use the World Wide Web to find, load, view, and create Web pages. Web browsers, like Netscape Navigator, Mosaic, and Cello, offer easy-to-use point-and-click environments for quickly accessing information on the Web. In other words, with a few simple mouse clicks, you can instantly find the best the World Wide Web has to offer. ▶ This textbook features the most popular Web browser, **Netscape Navigator 1.1 for Windows**, from Netscape Communications Corporation. Netscape is one of the newest Web browsers. It is faster and has more features than its predecessors. ▶ As the marketing manager for The Nut Tree, you recognize the many ways you could use Netscape Navigator to make your company more successful. With a Web browser you can:

■ **View Web pages that include graphics and text**
You can look at the Web pages of other companies to see how they are marketing their products on the Web.

■ **Navigate between Web pages**
You can browse the Web for ideas on impressive and persuasive Web page layouts to market The Nut Tree's products on-line.

■ **Search the Web**
You can use one of the many search methods to locate specific information on the Web that will be useful to you as you plan your on-line marketing strategy for The Nut Tree.

■ **Explore the categories of information on the Web**
You can view some of the many informational resources on the Web to learn more about issues important to Web users and to growing companies like The Nut Tree.

■ **Create your own Web pages**
You can build a custom Web page to market The Nut Tree's products on the World Wide Web.

FIGURE 1-1: Structure of the Internet

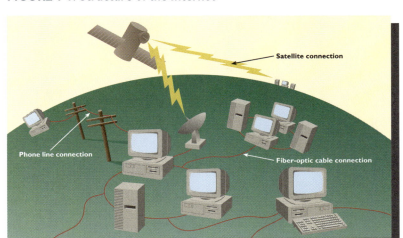

FIGURE 1-2: Structure of the Internet

Internet and World Wide Web history

The Internet came into existence during the 1960s, at the height of the Cold War. It was originally designed to withstand a nuclear attack. This network, called Arpanet, grew rapidly as many nonmilitary research institutions and universities began using it. In 1991, Congress passed legislation to expand the speed and capacity of the Internet further and opened it up to commercial usage.

About the same time, Tim Berners-Lee, an unknown researcher in Geneva at the European Particle Physics Laboratory (CERN), deployed the first components of the World Wide Web. In 1993, Marc Andreessen, then a student at the University of Illinois in Urbana-Champaign, introduced the first graphical Web browser, Mosaic. In 1994, the corporation Netscape Communications, co-owned by Marc Andreessen, introduced a Web browser called Netscape Navigator for Windows. This new browser was designed to work well in low-speed environments.

Starting Netscape Navigator 1.1

In this lesson you will find the Netscape application icon and start Netscape, using the Windows skills you developed in the "Working with Windows" section. The exact location of Netscape may vary on different computers. Hence, the steps you take to start Netscape might be different than those given below. See your instructor or technical support person for help if you are unable to locate the Netscape application icon. ▶ Before you can plan ways to market The Nut Tree's products on the Web, you need to start Netscape and explore its features.

1   Make sure the Program Manager window is open
The Program Manager icon might appear at the bottom of your screen. Double-click the icon to open it, if necessary.

2   Double-click the **Netscape program group icon**
The Netscape application icon appears in the Netscape program group, as shown in Figure 1-3. Depending on the applications installed on your computer, what you see on your screen might differ from the icons shown in this figure.

3   Double-click the **Netscape application icon**
Netscape opens and displays the *World Wide Web—Illustrated* home page, as shown in Figure 1-4. The home page is the first page Netscape loads when you launch the program.

FIGURE 1-3: Netscape program group

Netscape program group window

Netscape application icon

Your program groups might be different

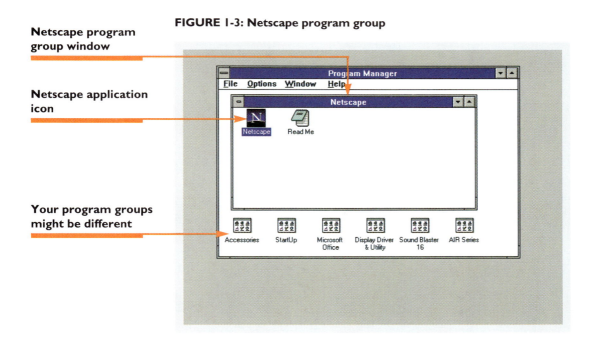

FIGURE 1-4: Home page for the *World Wide Web—Illustrated*

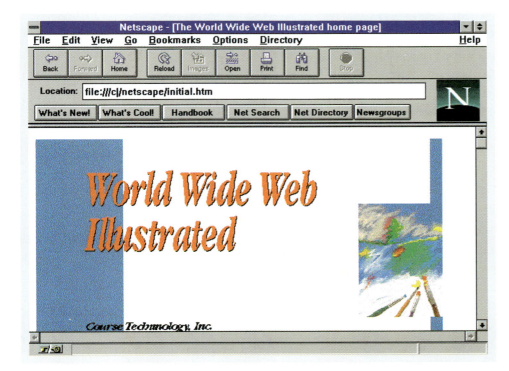

TROUBLE?

If your home page is missing or different from the one shown in Figure 1-4, ask your instructor or technical support person for assistance in getting to the correct home page.■

Exploring the Netscape window

When you start Netscape, the Netscape application window appears. The screen elements enable you to enter, view, and search for information. ▶ Begin your first day on the job at The Nut Tree exploring the Netscape environment. On your computer, locate each of the window elements with Figure 1-5 as your reference.

- A **Web page**, or **Web document**, is a specially formatted file designed for use on the World Wide Web. It lets you display information to anyone using the Web. A Web page typically includes text, graphics, and **links**, which when selected connect you to other Web pages. A Web page might also include sound and video clips if your computer has the appropriate hardware and software. The **title bar** displays the title of the current Web page.

- The **menu bar** displays the names of the menus that contain Netscape commands. When you click the name of a menu on the menu bar, a list of commands from which you can choose is displayed.

- The **toolbar** contains icons that act as shortcuts to activate frequently used menu commands.

- The **directory button bar** contains directory buttons that provide links connecting you to useful sites on the Web and the Internet.

- The **Location** or **Netsite text box** displays the address of the current page appearing in the document window. A **Web address**, or **Uniform Resource Locator (URL)**, is a unique string of text that identifies the location of a Web page on the World Wide Web.

- The **status indicator** (the Netscape Corporation's company logo) animates as a new page is loading. When the status indicator stops moving, the page loading process is complete.

- The **document window** displays the current Web page. Your **home page** is the initial Web page Netscape loads when you first launch the program.

- The **vertical** and **horizontal scroll bars** let you move quickly through a page. The **scroll box** in each scroll bar indicates your relative position in the page.

- The **progress bar** displays important information about the current operation, such as the percentage of a Web page layout and graphical display that is loaded during the loading process. The lower right box in the progress bar visually indicates the status of the page loading process by filling with a red bar.

- The **security indicator** shows if the Web page you are viewing is secured. A secure Web page means that you can safely transmit sensitive information, your credit card number for example . If the door key icon is displayed in blue, the information is secure. If the door key icon is broken and the background appears in grey, the Web document is not secured.

FIGURE 1-5: Elements of the Netscape application window

Menu bar

Location text box

Directory button bar

Document window

Web page

Security indicator

Progress bar

Title bar

Toolbar

Status indicator

Web address or URL

Vertical scroll bar

Scroll box

Horizontal scroll bar

TROUBLE?

If your Netscape application window does not cover your entire desktop, click the Maximize button.■

Working with menus, the toolbar, and directory buttons

Netscape often provides several ways to complete the same task using menus, the toolbar, or directory buttons. Although the menus in Netscape contain all the available commands and options, the toolbar and directory buttons, shown in Figure 1-6, offer a quicker and easier way to access frequently used commands and options. Tables 1-1 and 1-2 provide a brief description of the toolbar and directory buttons. ▶ You can use the Netscape Navigator controls to browse for more information on the World Wide Web. Familiarize yourself with these commands and options to learn how they can help you work more efficiently as you market The Nut Tree products on-line.

1. On the directory button bar, click the **Handbook button** [Handbook]
   The Netscape Handbook page appears, as shown in Figure 1-7.

2. Click the **Home button** [Home] in the toolbar
   Your original home page appears in the document window. Next open the Netscape Handbook using a menu command.

3. Click **Help** on the menu bar, then click **Handbook**
   The Netscape Handbook page once again appears in the document window.

4. Click **Go** on the menu bar, then click **Home**
   Your original home page appears in the document window. Directory buttons and toolbar buttons are easier to locate than menu commands, making them the most convenient way to navigate with your browser.

TABLE I-I: Toolbar buttons

TOOLBAR BUTTON NAME	BUTTON	DESCRIPTION
Back	Back	Displays previous page
Forward	Forward	Displays the next page in the series of pages already viewed
Home	Home	Displays your home (opening) page
Reload	Reload	Forces Netscape to completely reload a page
Images	Images	Loads images for the current page, if images are not loaded automatically
Open	Open	Allows the address of a Web page to be entered manually
Print	Print	Allows the printing of the current Web page
Find	Find	Locates text in a page based on the key word(s) specified
Stop	Stop	Halts the page loading process

FIGURE 1-6: Netscape controls

Menu bar

Toolbar

Directory button bar

FIGURE 1-7: Netscape Handbook page

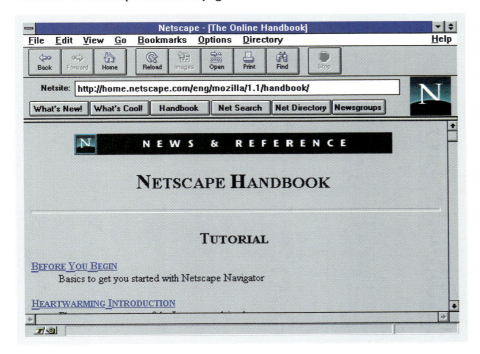

TROUBLE?

If the directory buttons are missing from your Netscape window, click Options on the menu bar, then click Show Directory Buttons. If the toolbar is missing from your Netscape window, click Options on the menu bar, then select Show Toolbar. Finally, if your toolbar is missing button names, you can use the Preferences command on the Options menu to open a Preferences dialog box. Choose the Styles option from the list box at the top of the dialog box. Click the Pictures and Text radio button, then click OK. To save these options, click Options on the menu bar, then click Save Options.■

TABLE 1-2: Directory buttons

DIRECTORY BUTTON NAME	BUTTON	DESCRIPTION
What's New!	What's New!	Displays a list of new Web pages
What's Cool!	What's Cool!	Displays a list of outstanding pages on the Web
Handbook	Handbook	Provides a guide to using Netscape
Net Search	Net Search	Allows searching of the Web based on key word(s)
Net Directory	Net Directory	Displays a subject-oriented listing of what's on the Web
Newsgroups	Newsgroups	Displays a page of newsgroups

Moving around a Web page

Netscape provides several convenient methods to scroll through longer pages. Although it is considered wise to keep Web pages short and concise for easy browsing, you will occasionally encounter a long page (e.g., directories, articles, etc.). Table 1-3 summarizes the ways you can move through a Web page. ▶ Practice moving through your home page, using a combination of these methods.

1 **Click the scroll down arrow at the bottom of the vertical scroll bar**
The document window scrolls down one inch to reveal new information at the bottom of the window.

2 **Click the scroll up arrow at the top of the vertical scroll bar**
The document window scrolls up one inch.

3 **Click below the scroll box in the vertical scroll bar**
The document window scrolls down the length of one window to display the next portion of your home page.

4 **Click above the scroll box in the vertical scroll bar**
The document window scrolls up the length of one window to show the previous view of the page.

5 **Drag the scroll box to the bottom of the vertical scroll bar**
The document window displays the bottom of the page, as shown in Figure 1-8. Notice the scroll box has moved to the bottom of the vertical scroll bar, indicating you have reached the end of the current Web page.

6 **Drag the scroll box to the top of the vertical scroll bar**
The document window displays the top of the page.

7 **Press [Ctrl][End]**
The bottom of the page appears in your document window.

8 **Press [Ctrl][Home]**
The top of the page appears in the document window.

FIGURE 1-8: Bottom of home page

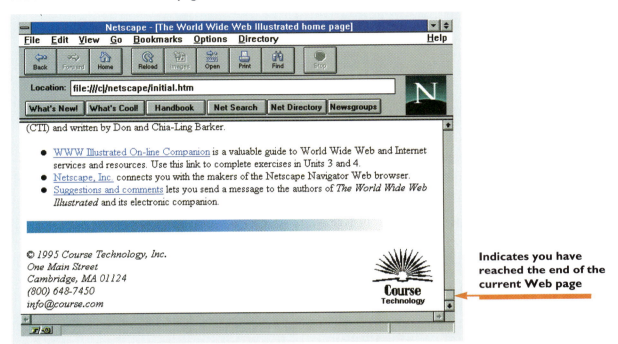

Indicates you have reached the end of the current Web page

TABLE 1-3: Methods for moving through a Web page

TO MOVE	CLICK OR PRESS
Down one inch	Down arrow in the vertical scroll bar or press [↓]
Up one inch	Up arrow in vertical scroll bar or press [↑]
Down one window	Below the scroll box in the vertical scroll bar or press [PgDn]
Up one window	Above the scroll box in the vertical scroll bar or press [PgUp]
To the top of the Web page	Press [Ctrl][Home]
To the end of the Web page	Press [Ctrl][End]

Getting Help

Netscape uses an on-line Help system that provides information and instructions on Netscape features and commands while you are using Netscape. Table 1-4 describes the Help commands available in the Help menu. ▶ As the new Marketing Manager for The Nut Tree, you want to find out more about what Netscape can do. Use the Frequently Asked Questions (FAQs) command in the Help menu to view the type of help available.

I **Click Help on the menu bar**
The Help menu appears, as shown in Figure 1-9.

2 **Click Frequently Asked Questions**
The document window displays a Web page, as shown in Figure 1-10. This is an on-line Help feature, which means Netscape Communications Corporation updates this information on a regular basis. Your document window might therefore look different from the one shown in the figure.

3 **Scroll down the page and study its contents**

4 **When you are done looking at this page, click the Home button** **on the toolbar**
Your home page reappears in the document window.

TABLE 1-4: Help Menu

COMMAND	PROVIDES
About Netscape...	Version and copyright information
Registration Information	Information on registering your copy of Netscape
Handbook	Tutorial on using Netscape
Release Notes	Latest information on Netscape
Frequently Asked Questions	Answers to common questions from Netscape users
On Security	Information on the security scheme used in Netscape
How to Give Feedback	Instructions on how to send comments to Netscape
How to Get Support	Instructions on how to register and get support for your copy of Netscape
How to Create Web Services	Resources for creating your own Web pages and Web server

FIGURE I-9: Help menu in Netscape

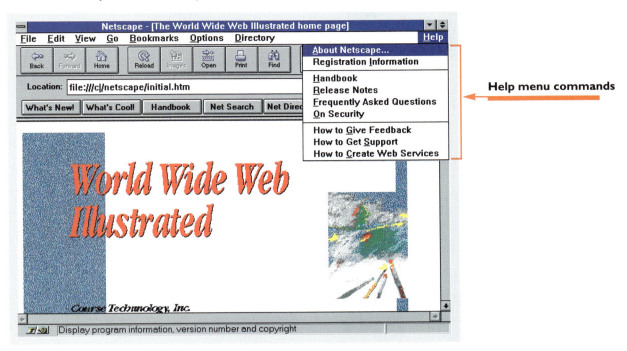

Help menu commands

FIGURE I-10: Frequently Asked Questions page

Home button

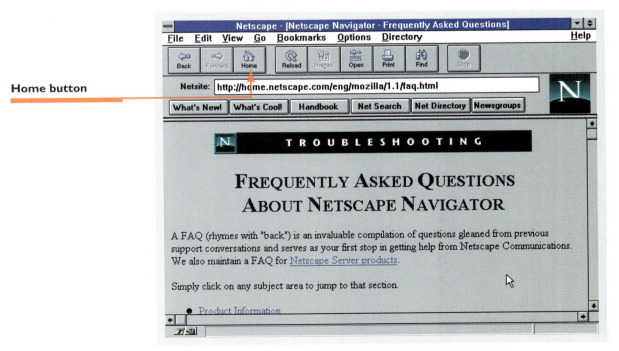

Printing a Web page

You can print the current Web page (i.e., the one displayed in your document window) by simply selecting the Print button on the toolbar, specifying the print options you want in the Print dialog box, and clicking the OK button. The Print dialog box lets you specify the number of copies and the page ranges you want to print. Table 1-5 provides additional information on all the Netscape printing options. ▶ Melissa Shea, the owner of The Nut Tree, has never used the Internet or the World Wide Web. She has asked to see a printout of what a home page looks like. Use the Print dialog box to print two copies of your home page—one for Melissa and one for your records.

1 Click **File** on the menu bar, then click **Print**
The Print dialog box appears, as shown in Figure 1-11.

2 Double-click the **Copies text box**, and type **2**
The Copies text box changes to display two copies to be printed. If you accidentally indicate a different number of copies, repeat Step 2 to correct the mistake. (Note: This number of copies becomes the default number to print until you either exit Netscape or change the number.)

3 Make sure your printer is turned on, is on-line, and contains paper

4 Click **OK**
The Print dialog box closes and the current Web page prints.

FIGURE 1-11: Print dialog box

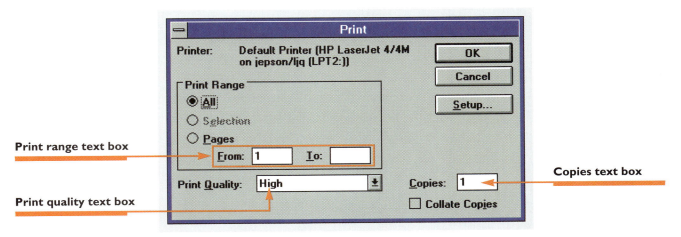

Print range text box

Print quality text box

Copies text box

TABLE 1-5: Printing options

OPTIONS	DESCRIPTION
Printer	Displays the name of active printer
Print range	Indicates the pages to print *All* prints the entire document *Selection* prints the portions of the document you select *Pages* prints the pages you specify
Print Quality	Specifies the dots per inch or resolution to be used
Copies	Indicates the number of copies to print
Collate Copies	Prints all the pages of the document in sequence

Exiting Netscape

When you are ready to exit Netscape, you select the Exit command on the File menu. Unlike many other Windows applications, there is no need to save documents before exiting Netscape. Netscape Navigator lets you only view documents, not create or edit them. Therefore, you can exit the program without closing the document window. See the related topic "Opening and closing multiple Netscape document windows" in this lesson for more information on closing Web documents. ▶ You have completed your first day as the marketing manager for The Nut Tree. Exit Netscape Navigator before leaving the office.

1 Click **File** on the menu bar
The File menu opens, as shown in Figure 1-12.

2 Click **Exit** on the File menu
The Netscape application window closes, and you return to Program Manager.

FIGURE 1-12: Netscape application window with File menu open

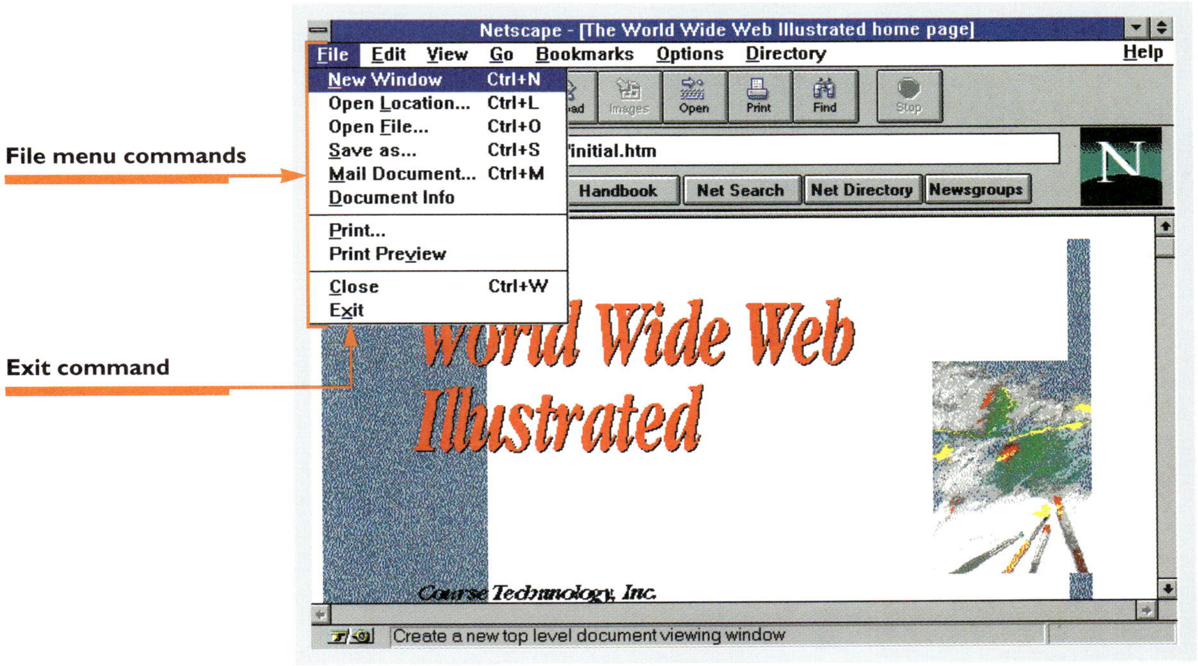

File menu commands

Exit command

Opening and closing multiple Netscape document windows

You can use the New Window command on the File menu to open another instance of the Netscape application window when you want to display multiple Web pages simultaneously. If you want to close one of the Web pages without closing the others, choose the Close command on the File menu of the page you want to close. To close all open pages at once, simply select Exit from the File menu of any Netscape application window.

QUICK **TIP**

You can also exit from Netscape by double-clicking the control menu box in the left-hand corner of the title bar of the Netscape application window.■

TASKREFERENCE

TASK	MOUSE/BUTTON	MENU	KEYBOARD
Start Netscape 1.1	Double-click Netscape program group icon, then double-click Netscape application icon		[Alt] [W] using arrow keys to select Netscape [Enter]
Maximize Netscape Application window	▲	Click the **Control menu box**, then click **Maximize**	[Alt] [Spacebar] [X]
Return to Home Page	🏠 Home	Click **Go, Home**	[Alt] [G] [H]
Show Directory Buttons		Click **Options**, **Show Directory Buttons**	[Alt] [O] [D]
Show Toolbar		Click **Options**, **Show Toolbar**	[Alt] [O] [T]
Show Button Names		Click **Options**, **Preferences**, in Preference dialog box, choose **Styles**, then click **Pictures** and **Text**, **OK**	[Alt] [O] [P] [Tab] [Tab] [Tab] using arrow keys to select the Text Box [Enter]
Move down the Web page one inch	⬇		⬇
Move up the Web page one inch	⬆		⬆
Move down one window	Click below scroll box		[PgDn]
Move up one window	Click above scroll box		[PgUp]
Move to top of Web page	Drag scroll box to top of vertical scroll bar		[Ctrl] [Home]
Move to bottom of	Drag scroll box to bottom of vertical scroll bar		[Ctrl] [End]Web page
Access Help		Click **Help**	[Alt] [H]
Print a document	🖨 Print	Click **File**, **Print**	[Alt] [F] [P]
Preview a document		Click **File**, **Print Preview**	[Alt] [F] [V]
Exit Netscape	Double-click Netscape control menu box	Click **File**, **Exit**	[Alt] [F] [X]

CONCEPTSREVIEW

Label each of the elements of the Netscape application window in Figure 1-13.

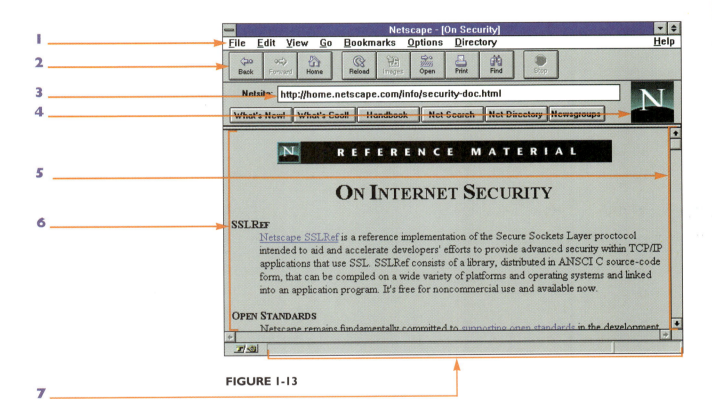

FIGURE 1-13

Match each of the terms below with the statement that best describes its function.

8 Toolbar

9 Scroll bar

10 Document window

11 Location text box

12 Status indicator

a. Displays a Web page

b. Indicates Netscape is loading a page

c. Contains shortcuts to menu commands

d. Indicates the address of the current page

e. Contains controls for moving through a document

Select the best answer from the list of choices.

13 A Web browser lets you

a. Create Web pages

b. Explore binary files on your hard disk

c. View pages on the Web

d. Browse non-ASCII files at remote sites

14 To view another part of a Web page

a. Click the Relocate button on the toolbar

b. Move the scroll box in the scroll bar

c. Drag the toolbar

d. Select the Leap command from the Navigate menu

15 To go to the top of a document

   a. Drag the scroll box to the top of the scroll bar

   b. Press [Ctrl][Top]

   c. Click the Home button on the toolbar

   d. Double-click the scroll bar

16 You can get Netscape Help by

   a. Clicking Help in the menu bar

   b. Pressing the F1 function key

   c. Clicking the Help button on the toolbar

   d. Pressing [Alt][Help]

17 What key(s) do you press to move down a Web page?

   a. [End]

   b. [PgDn]

   c. [Shift][End]

   d. [Enter][End]

18 You can print a document in Netscape in any of the following ways *except*

   a. Click the Print button on the toolbar

   b. Click File, click Print, then click OK

   c. Click File, click Print Preview, then click Print

   d. Press [Alt][FP] and then [Enter]

19 The directory button bar lets you do all of the following *except*

   a. Print a Web page

   b. Search the Web

   c. See what's new

   d. Read newsgroups

20 _____was the military network that eventually developed into what is today known as the Internet.

   a. Arpanet

   b. MilNet

   c. CERN

   d. WebNet

21 Who introduced the first graphical Web browser?

   a. Tim Berners-Lee

   b. Mark Andreessen

   c. Don Barker

   d. Jeffrey Jones

22 Your home page is

   a. a Web page detailing information about your computer

   b. the initial Web page Netscape loads whenever you launch the program

   c. a page you create to tell other Web users about yourself

   d. a Web page devoted to the realty business

23 URL stands for

   a. Universal Requester List

   b. Uniform Resource List

   c. Uniform Resource Locator

   d. Universal Regional Locator

24 The first graphical Web browser was

   a. Netscape Navigator

   b. Arpanet

   c. Surf

   d. Mosaic

25 You can exit Netscape by

   a. double-clicking Netscape's control menu box

   b. clicking Exit on the File menu

   c. [Alt][F][X]

   d. all of the above

26 A Web page that is secured will have the following characteristic

   a. a blue door key icon

   b. the word SECURE in bold across the top of it

   c. a blue padlock icon

   d. a red title bar

APPLICATIONS
REVIEW

1 Start Netscape and identify elements of the application window.

   a. Make sure the computer is on and Windows is running.

   b. Double-click the Netscape program group icon.

   c. Double-click the Netscape application icon.

   d. Without referring to the lesson material, identify the toolbar, the menu bar, the directory button bar, the scroll bars, the location text box, the status indicator, and the progress bar in the Netscape application window.

2 Explore the Netscape menus, the toolbar, and directory buttons.

   a. Click Edit on the menu bar, then click Find to open the Find dialog box. This dialog box lets you locate text in a Web page that matches the text you enter in this dialog box. Close the dialog box by clicking the Cancel button.

   b. Open the Find dialog box by clicking the Find button on the toolbar, then close it again by selecting the Cancel button in the dialog box.

   c. Click the What's New! directory button. Once the What's New! page has loaded in the document window, click the Home button on the toolbar to return to your home page.

   d. Click Directory on the menu bar, then click What's New! Once the What's New! page has loaded in the document window, click the Home button on the toolbar to return to your home page.

   e. Try some of the other directory buttons and directory commands. When you finish, select the Home button on the toolbar.

3 Move around the document window.

   a. Click the scroll down arrow in the vertical scroll bar twice.

   b. Click the scroll up arrow in the vertical scroll bar twice.

   c. Click below the scroll box in the vertical scroll bar.

   d. Click above the scroll box in the vertical scroll bar.

   e. Drag the scroll box to the bottom of the vertical scroll bar.

4 Explore Netscape Help.

   a. Click Help on the menu bar.

   b. Click one of the commands in the Help menu.

   c. Once the Help page opens, read the document.

   d. Select another option on the Help menu, read the Help information on that topic, then close the window and return to the home page by clicking the Home button on the toolbar.

5 Print a Web page.

   a. Click the What's New! directory button.

   b. When the What's New! page finishes loading in the document window, click File on the menu bar, then click Print.

   c. To print just the first page of this Web document, click the Pages radio button in the Print Range area of the Print dialog box.

   d. Then press [Tab] and type "1" in the "To" text box, then click OK.

6 Preview a Web page, then print the page and exit Netscape.

   a. Click the Home button.

   b. Click the WWW Illustrated Online Companion link.

   c. To see how the current Web page will look when printed, click File and then click Print Preview. Netscape formats the document for printing and displays it.

   d. If the Web page is longer than a single printed page, click the Next Page button at the top of the Print Preview window to display another page. (The Zoom In and Zoom Out buttons allow you to examine in detail any portion of a Web page.)

   e. Click the Print button then click OK to print the Web page. (The Close button returns you to the document window without printing the Web page.)

   f. When the page is printed, click File on the menu bar, and then click Exit.

INDEPENDENT
CHALLENGE 1

Write a short essay on what you hope to learn from this book. Be sure to include a section on how you think Netscape and the World Wide Web will help you in your academic/professional life. You can use any word processor to write and print this essay. If you are unfamiliar with a word processor, use Notepad, a simple text processor included with Microsoft Windows 3.1 in the Accessories work group.

INDEPENDENT
CHALLENGE 2

Use your library to find several articles on how the World Wide Web might impact businesses. Write a brief summary of the articles. You can use any word processor to write and print the summary. If you are unfamiliar with a word processor, use Notepad, a simple text processor included with Microsoft Windows 3.1 in the Accessories work group.

UNIT 2

Navigating
THE WEB

Now that you are familiar with Netscape's toolbar, menus, dialog boxes, and Help system, you are ready to navigate the Web. In this unit, you will learn how easy it is to move between Web pages. Netscape provides a powerful set of tools that let you control what you view on the World Wide Web. ▶ As the on-line marketing manager for The Nut Tree, you firmly believe that the Web represents an attractive medium for marketing the firm's products. However, before making any recommendations to Melissa Shea, the owner of the company, you want to become adept at moving around the Web. ▶

Understanding hypertext links and URLs

Think of the World Wide Web as a very large book or encyclopedia of information. Each page in this encyclopedia is referred to as a **Web page**. Each page in this encyclopedia may contain one or more hypertext links. **Hypertext links**, **hyperlinks**, or just **links**, enable you to open related Web pages by clicking them with your mouse. You can use these links to follow a topic from page to page through the encyclopedia without regard to where or in what order the pages reside. ▶ To distinguish links from the other text in a Web page, links are highlighted in a special color and underlined. See the related topic "Other hypermedia" for a description of the other ways links may appear in a Web page. Figure 2-1 shows a Web page with several links. If you wanted to find information on the newest companies selling gift packages of assorted nuts and confectioneries, you could click the link <u>Sweets and Snacks</u>. Your browser then would locate the related Web page using its **URL**, or **Uniform Resource Locator**. Using the encyclopedia analogy, a Web page's URL would be equivalent to its page number. For example, the URL address for the Web page shown in Figure 2-1 is http://www.mecklerweb.com/imall/food.htm. Each Web page has a URL , which serves as its address within the World Wide Web. ▶ Once the Sweets and Snacks page opens, you can click the name of a company shown in a list on that Web page to move to a Web page profiling that specific company. ▶ There are several components that make up a URL. Each of these components is described in detail below.

■ The acronym HTTP (HyperText Transport Protocol) is found in each URL. **HTTP** is the communication standard or protocol established for the World Wide Web. It ensures that everybody is talking the same language when sending and receiving Web pages.

A colon and two forward slashes (e.g., http://) indicate that the Web page is located on a remote Web site.

■ The name of the Web site typically begins with the three letters "www" (e.g., www.mecklerweb.com), signifying that the location belongs to the World Wide Web. The second part of the site name is called the **domain name** (e.g., mecklerweb.com). The first component of the domain name (e.g., mecklerweb) usually stands for the name of the institution that owns the site. (In this case, mecklerweb stands for Meckler Media.) A **Web site**, or **server**, is a computer or a network of computers that makes pages available on the Web. The final three letters, or **top-level domain**, (e.g., .com) tell you the kind of site or institution you are dealing with. In this example, .com indicates that this is a commercial site. Table 2-1 lists some common top-level domains.

FIGURE 2-1: Hypertext links in Web pages

Web site

URL address

Hypertext links

Other hypermedia

Links to other Web pages can also appear as images. Images, or graphics, in Web pages might contain **hyperregions** you can click to view related pages. For example, a Web page might display a picture of our solar system with nine planets. Each planet could be a hyperregion that, when clicked, would open a page of information about that planet. Since these graphical links are easy to understand, you'll find that many Web pages offer images with hyperregions to simplify navigation.

TABLE 2-1: Common top-level domains

TOP-LEVEL DOMAIN	LOCATION	TOP-LEVEL DOMAIN	LOCATION
au	Australia	gov	Government agencies
ca	Canada	int	International organizations
com	Commercial sites	mil	Military
edu	Educational institutions	net	Network organizations
es	Spain	org	Nonprofit organizations
fr	France	uk	United Kingdom

Finding, starting, and stopping links

To make links easily recognizable, they are always highlighted in a color different from the rest of the text on a Web page. Once you select a link, it changes color again to indicate that you have chosen it. Unselected, or **unfollowed**, links are blue by default, while links that have already been selected, or **followed**, are purple. By changing the color of a link, Netscape provides a clear marker to help you keep track of where you have been on the World Wide Web. ▶ To select a link in a Web page, simply click it. Netscape will then attempt to locate and **load** (open) the page using its URL address. However, because the Web runs over the Internet, with thousands of sites connected by thousands of networks, things can go wrong when you try to load a page. If your browser seems to be taking a very long time to locate and/or load a page, you can interrupt the operation by clicking the Stop button on the toolbar. This will halt the loading operation and return control of the browser to you. ▶ Netscape will continue to display the current page in the document window up to the point when a new page begins loading. If you have selected the Stop button, the document window will display the portion of the page Netscape was able to load before the load operation was halted. ▶ Begin your quest for information on how other companies use the Web as a marketing tool by selecting a link from your home page.

1   Start Netscape, and scroll through your home page until you locate the link WWW Illustrated Online Companion
    Notice that when you move the mouse pointer over the link, the pointer ▨ changes to a hand 👆. This is yet another indication that this is a hypertext link.

2   Click the link **WWW Illustrated Online Companion**
    After a moment, the status indicator stops moving and the document window displays the WWW Illustrated Online Companion, as shown in Figure 2-2. This page provides an extensive guide to sites on the Web and is designed to be used in concert with your textbook. You want to select a link from this page that will lead you to Web pages providing information on other companies selling products and services on the Web.

3   Scroll through the Web page until you reach the link Exploring the Web, then click the link **Exploring business**, which is indented under this heading
    A new Web page opens, displaying links to various business resources on the Web.

4   Scroll down to the heading *Shopping* and click one of the links appearing below the *Malls* heading, such as the **marketplaceMCI** link, then as the new Web page begins to load, click the **Stop button** 🔴 Stop on the toolbar

    Netscape halts the process of finding and loading the linked page. If you click the Stop button too soon, your document window may be empty. Just click the Reload button on the toolbar to restart the loading process and wait until the page begins to appear before clicking the Stop button. If you receive an error message, click OK and try this step again.

FIGURE 2-2: WWW Illustrated Online Companion page

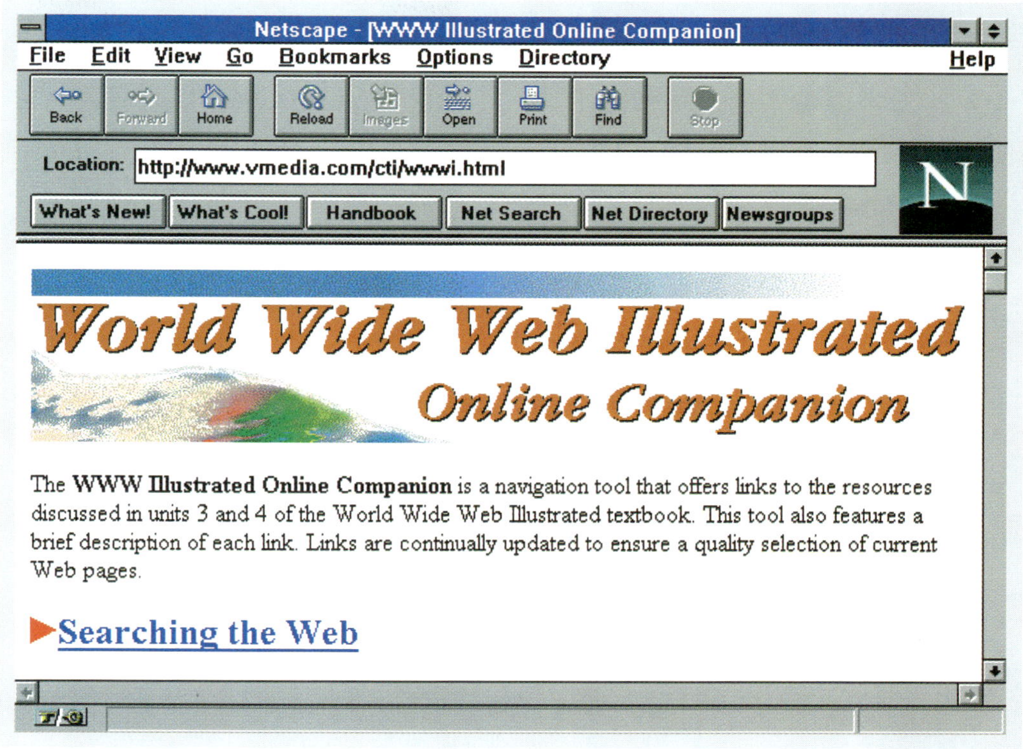
Netscape - [WWW Illustrated Online Companion]
File Edit View Go Bookmarks Options Directory Help
Back
Forward
Home
Reload
Images
Open
Print
Find
Stop
Location: http://www.vmedia.com/cti/wwwi.html
What's New!
What's Cool!
Handbook
Net Search
Net Directory
Newsgroups
N
World Wide Web Illustrated
Online Companion
The WWW Illustrated Online Companion is a navigation tool that offers links to the resources discussed in units 3 and 4 of the World Wide Web Illustrated textbook. This tool also features a brief description of each link. Links are continually updated to ensure a quality selection of current Web pages.
Searching the Web

TROUBLE?

If your home page does not contain the link **WWW Illustrated Online Companion**, check with your instructor or technical support person.

Moving backward and forward

Netscape makes it easy to navigate backward and forward through Web pages you have previously viewed. Selecting the Back button on the toolbar displays the previous page you visited in your document window. Choosing the Forward button sends you to the next page in the series of pages you have been viewing. See the related topic "Going Home" to learn how to quickly and easily return to your home page at any time, no matter where you are on the Web. ▶ Melissa Shea was impressed by the list of electronic malls and storefronts you found in the previous lesson. Now that you see how widely the Web is used by other organizations as a marketing tool, you need to find out how to get The Nut Tree company and product information on the Web. Use the Back and Forward buttons to return to the WWW Illustrated Online Companion page to look for another link that may provide the information you are looking for.

1 Click the **Back button** [Back] on the toolbar once
The previously viewed page appears in your document window.

2 Click the **Back button** [Back] twice
Your home page appears in the document window. Notice the Back button is now grayed out to indicate that you have reached the first page viewed and that this button is temporarily unavailable for use. See Figure 2-3.

3 Click the **Forward button** [Forward] once
The WWW Illustrated Online Companion page appears, as shown in Figure 2-4. Notice the Back and Forward buttons are not grayed out.

FIGURE 2-3: Your home page

The Back button is grayed out to indicate it is inactive

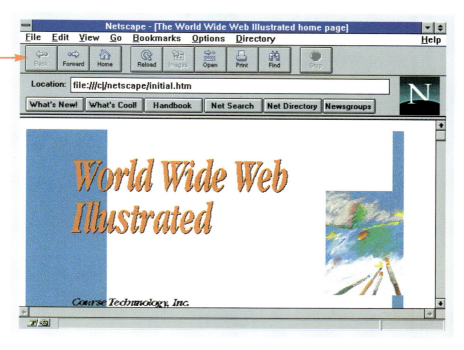

FIGURE 2-4: WWW Illustrated Online Companion page

Back and Forward buttons both active

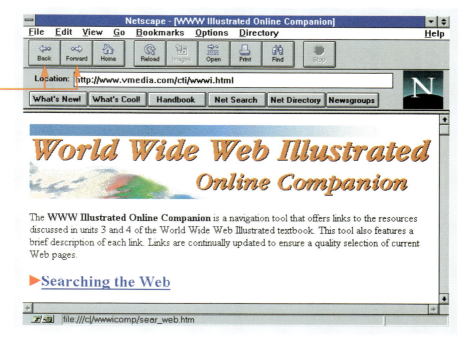

Going Home

The Home button on the toolbar lets you immediately return to your home page from any location on the Web. (The Home command on the Go menu performs the same function.) This is a very handy feature because it is easy to get lost in the many linked pages, often called **strands**, of the Web.

Viewing history

Netscape offers another way to move among previously selected Web pages with its View History option. Instead of using the Back and Forward buttons to search for a previously viewed page, you can go straight to it by selecting View History on the Go menu and then selecting the name of any previously viewed page. ▶ Use the View History option to review the Web pages you have already visited to make sure you didn't overlook anything of value.

1   Click **Go** on the menu bar

Note that the Go menu displays a list of the pages you have visited, with the most recent page at the top of the list. At times you will want a more complete picture of where you have been. The View History command will open a dialog box that can display a very lengthy list of Web pages.

2   Click the **View History** command

A History dialog box opens, as shown in Figure 2-5. If other Web pages have been viewed recently with your browser, your list may be considerably longer than the one pictured in the figure. The name of the most recently viewed page appears at the top of the list box. This list runs from the most recent page visited to the oldest at the bottom. Table 2-2 provides a brief description of the options in the History dialog box.

3   Click **Exploring business**

The Exploring business Web page is highlighted.

4   Click the **Go to button**

The History dialog box remains open, and the document window behind it changes to display the Exploring business page viewed previously.

5   Click the **Close button** to close the History dialog box

The History dialog box closes, and the Exploring business page is in full view. The choices on this page all seem too broad to satisfy your need for information on marketing on the Web. In the next lesson, try to navigate more directly to a page on this topic using the Find button.

FIGURE 2-5: History dialog box

Last page viewed

First page viewed

Your list might
be different

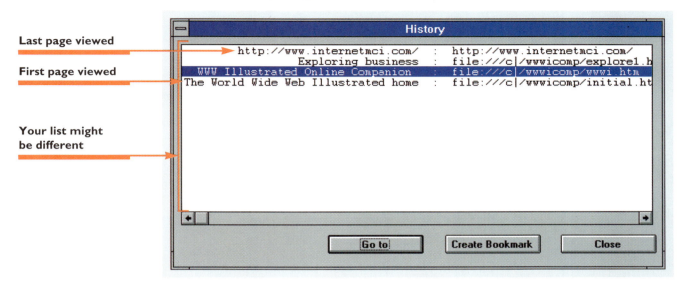

TABLE 2-2: Options in the History dialog box

BUTTON	DESCRIPTION
Go to	Opens the page currently selected in the History dialog box
Create Bookmark	Adds the currently selected page to your Bookmark List, which you will learn about later in this unit
Close	Closes the History dialog box

QUICK TIP

The second time you visit the same site, Netscape automatically removes the first visit from your History list.■

Finding text

Sometimes you will want to find a specific word or phrase in a Web page. Scrolling through the page and trying to spot text can be a very haphazard and time-consuming process. Netscape provides a Find button on the toolbar to automate this process. ▶ You are searching for information on how to market products on the Web, so use the Find button to search the Web page for occurrences of the word "market."

1 Make sure the Exploring business page is open, and click the **Find button** 🔍 on the toolbar

The Find dialog box appears, as shown in Figure 2-6. Table 2-3 lists all the options found in the Find dialog box.

2 Click the **Find What text box** and type **market**

The word "market" appears in the text box.

3 Click the **Find Next button**

The document window changes to show the portion of the page with the first instance of "market." You may need to move the Find dialog box to a different position to see the first instance of "market" highlighted on the Web page.

4 Click the **Find Next button** again

The second occurrence of "market" in this page appears highlighted in the document window.

5 Click the **Find Next button** once more

Yet another instance of "market" is found.

6 Continue to click the **Find Next button** until you receive the message "Search String Not Found!" and then click the **OK** button

Netscape has now searched the entire page from top to bottom.

7 Click the **Cancel button** in the Find dialog box to close it

The last instance of "market" remains highlighted after closing the Find dialog box.

FIGURE 2-6: The Find dialog box

Type word or
phrase you are
searching for here

Click here to
initiate search

Match Case check box

Direction search
will take you through
Web page

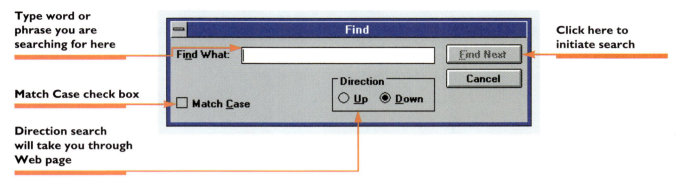

TABLE 2-3: Find dialog box options

OPTION	DESCRIPTION
Find What text box	Allows the entry of keywords to search for
Find Next button	Locates and highlights the next occurrence of text in a Web page that matches the entry in the Find What text box
Cancel button	Closes the Find dialog box
Match Case check box	When selected, causes Netscape to search for text that exactly matches the capitalization used in the Find What text box
Up radio button	Searches the Web page from the insertion point up for a match to the entry in the Find What text box
Down radio button	Searches the Web page from the insertion point down for a match to the entry in the Find What text box

QUICK

You can also click
Edit on the menu bar,
and then click Find to
locate a specific word
or phrase in a Web
page.■

Using bookmarks

Netscape provides a convenient feature, called a **Bookmark List**, that lets you collect Web pages of interest and easily revisit them any time. To add a bookmark to the list, simply display the page you want in the document window and select the Add Bookmark command on the Bookmarks menu. The related topic "Organizing your bookmarks" describes some ways of categorizing a long bookmark list. ▶ As on-line marketing manager of The Nut Tree, you think the Exploring business page will be a useful resource as you plan to put information about your company on the Web. Create a bookmark for this page so you can easily return to it.

1   Make sure the Exploring business page is displayed in your document window, click **Bookmarks** on the menu bar, then click **Add Bookmark**
The name and URL of the Exploring business page are added to the bookmark list.

2   Click the **Home button**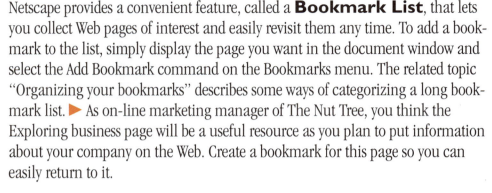
Your home page appears in the document window.

3   Click **Bookmarks** on the menu bar, then click **View Bookmarks**
The Bookmark List dialog box opens with the latest bookmarks displayed at the bottom of the bookmark list, as shown in Figure 2-7. (You may need to scroll down the list.) See Table 2-4 for a description of the dialog box options.

4   Click **Exploring business** in the list box, then click the **Go To button**
The Bookmark List dialog box remains open, and the document window displays the Exploring business page behind it.

5   Click the **Close button**, then click the **Home button**

TABLE 2-4: Bookmark List dialog box options

OPTION	DESCRIPTION
Add Bookmark button	Adds the name and URL address of the current page to the list
Go To button	Loads the selected page into the document window
Up button	Moves the currently selected page name up the list
Down button	Moves the currently selected page down the list
Find button	Initiates a search of the list for a page name that matches the name entered in the Find text box
Find text box	Lets you enter the name of a page to search for in the list
Edit button	Displays an extension to the Bookmark List dialog box that lets you organize your bookmark list with headings, descriptions, and modified page names
Close button	Closes the Bookmark List dialog box

FIGURE 2-7: Bookmark List dialog box

New bookmark added

Organizing your bookmarks

As your bookmark list grows, you'll find organizing the page names into categories (e.g., business, education, electronic publishing, entertainment, etc.) will make it easier to locate the page you want. Start by opening the Bookmark List dialog box and selecting a page name. Use the Up and Down buttons in the dialog box to move the name right below another page name in the same category (e.g. electronic publishing). Continue arranging your page names until all of them are grouped into categories.

Then use the Edit button in the dialog box to display the editing features available for the bookmark list. These editing features enable you to label your categories with header names. Your header name will appear in the main list, with a hyphen in front of it to signify that the item is a header and not a Web page listing. Repeat this process for each category grouping to organize your entire bookmark list. Close the Bookmark List when you are done. For a complete description of all the editing features in the Bookmark List dialog box, check the Netscape Handbook by clicking the Handbook button.

QUICK **TIP**

If your Bookmark menu exceeds Netscape's capacity to display them, you can choose the More Bookmarks option at the bottom of the Bookmark menu to display the Bookmark List dialog box.■

TROUBLE?

If you are working in a lab, it might be necessary to remove the bookmarks you've added in this lesson. To delete bookmarks, click the Edit button in the Bookmark List dialog box, click a bookmark you added in the bookmark list, then click the Remove Item button.■

Entering a URL address

Links make navigating the Web as simple as pointing and clicking. However, when you want to view a page without a readily available link, you will need to enter manually the location of the page, which is its URL. The Open button on the tool-bar provides a dialog box for entering a URL address manually. ▶ Your marketing assistant found a list of Web sites for popular confectionary companies in a maga-zine. She made a list of the URLs for The Nut Tree's competitors' pages, as shown in Table 2-5. Use the URL address for the Krema Nut Company, The Nut Tree's number one competitor, to view their Web page.

I Click the **Open button** [Open] on the toolbar
The Open Location dialog box appears, as shown in Figure 2-8.

2 Type **http://www.infinet.com/~schapman/krema.html** in the Open Location text box, then click the **Open** button in the dialog box
The status indicator animates, and after a brief time the Krema Nut Company Web page appears, as pictured in Figure 2-9. Once you have explored this page and some of its links, continue on with the next step. (If you receive an error while trying to open the Krema Nut Company page, use the Open Location dialog box to enter another URL listed in Table 2-5.)

3 Click the **Open button** [Open] on the toolbar again
The Open Location dialog box displays the URL you entered earlier. You can use your edit keys to modify this address rather than typing in an entire new URL.

4 Click at the end of the previous URL address in the Open Location text box
A flashing insertion point (text cursor) appears at the end of the URL.

5 Press **[Backspace]** as many times as necessary to erase everything back to the first forward slash
The Open Location dialog box now displays only the beginning of a URL address, http://.

6 Be sure the cursor is positioned after the second forward slash, then type **www.godiva.com/**, and then click **Open**
Once more the status indicator animates and, after a brief time, the document window displays the initial page at the Godiva Chocolatier company.

7 Click the **Home button** [Home] on the toolbar
The document window displays your home page.

8 Exit Netscape

FIGURE 2-8: Open Location dialog box

Type the URL of the
Web page you wish
to view here

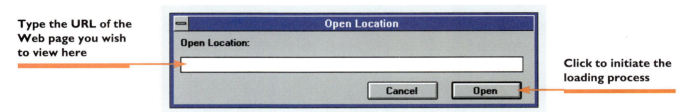

Click to initiate the
loading process

FIGURE 2-9: The Krema Nut Company Web page

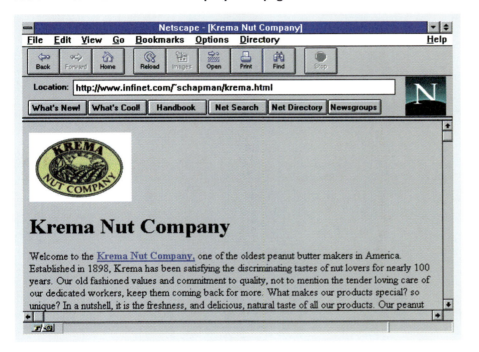

QUICK **TIP**

Uniform Resource
Locator addresses are
case sensitive. So,
always enter the upper-
case and lowercase
letters in a URL exactly
as shown. Otherwise,
your attempt to load a
Web page may result in
an error message
telling you that the pro-
gram was unable to find
the specified URL.■

TABLE 2-5: URLs of potential competitors of The Nut Tree

COMPANY NAME	URL
Ann Hemyng Candy's Chocolate Factory	http://mmink.com/mmink/dossiers/choco.html
Barbra Jean's Famous Candies	http://sashimi.wwa.com:80/bjcandy/
Couture Maple Syrup Products	http://www.pbpub.com/~tbpb/couture.htm
Five Star Cookie Company	http://www.virtumall.com/LateNightCookies/FiveStar.html
Goodies from Goodman	http://www.branch.com:80/goodies/
Griffin Chocolates	http://www.branch.com.80/chocolate/
Krema Nut Company	http://www.infinet.com/~schapman/krema.html
Rowena's Baked Goods	http://emall.com/Rowena/Rowena1.html

TASKREFERENCE

TASK	MOUSE/BUTTON	MENU	KEYBOARD
Start a hypertext link	Click underlined or highlighted text, or graphic	Click Go, Home	[Alt][G][H]
Stop a link	Click [Stop]		[Esc]
Move back a link	Click [Back]	Click Go, Back	[Alt][G][B]
Move forward a link	Click [Forward]	Click Go, Forward	[Alt][G][F]
Go to Home page	Click [Home]	Click Go, Home	[Alt][G][H]
View History		Click Go, View History	[Ctrl][H]
Find text	Click [Find], type text, click Find Next	Click Edit, Find	[Ctrl][F]
Create Bookmarks		Click Bookmarks, Add Bookmark	[Ctrl][A]
View Bookmarks		Click Bookmarks, View Bookmarks	[Ctrl][B]
Edit Bookmarks		Click Bookmarks, View Bookmarks, Edit	
Enter a URL	Click [Open], type URL, click Open	Click File, Open Location	[Ctrl][L]

CONCEPTSREVIEW

Label each of the elements of the Bookmark List dialog box shown in Figure 2-10.

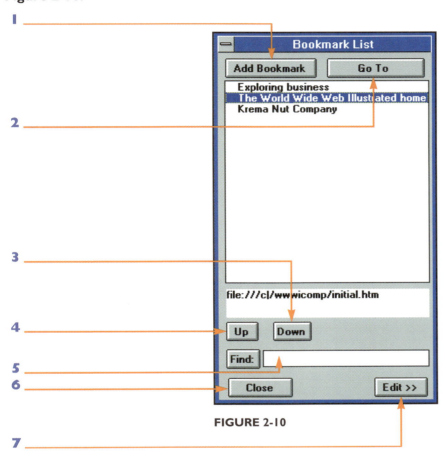

FIGURE 2-10

Match each of the terms below with the statement that best describes it function.

8 Add Bookmark button

9 Forward button

10 URL

11 Home button

12 Back button

a. Returns you to your home page

b. Loads the previously viewed page

c. Collects the name and location of pages

d. Jumps to the next page in a previously viewed series of pages

e. Address of a Web page

Select the best answer from the list of choices.

13 A link in a Web page lets you

a. Jump to another Web page

b. Connect two hyperzones

c. Load your home page

d. Create linkages that never fail

14 To view the previous page

a. Click the Hyper Reverse button

b. Click the Back button

c. Click the Previous command on the Go menu

d. Select the Backup command on the Go menu

15 The Bookmark List dialog box lets you do everything *except*

   a. Edit the page name

   b. Add the current page to the list

   c. Remove an entry from the list

   d. Move a page around the Web

16 The History dialog box lets you do everything *except*

   a. Delete an item from the History list

   b. Go to an item listed in the History dialog box

   c. Create a bookmark for the selected page

   d. Close the dialog box

17 Which of the following buttons allow you to search for text in a page?

   a. Search

   b. LookUp

   c. Find

   d. Locate

18 Which URL address in *incorrect*?

   a. http://www.company.com

   b. http://www.company.com/home.html

   c. http://www.company/home.html

   d. http://www.company.com/homepage.html

19 HTTP stands for

   a. HyperText Translate Protocol

   b. HyperText Transfer Pilot

   c. HyperText Transport Protocol

   d. HyperText Transport Pointer

20 _____ is the second part of a Web site's name and tells you the name of the Web site and the type of institution it is.

   a. top-level domain

   b. domain name

   c. origin name

   d. URL

21 The top-level domain, .ca, means the Web site you are accessing is

   a. located in California

   b. located in Canada

   c. a commercial site

   d. contains information on all types of candy

22 A link you have previously selected, or followed, appears on the screen in

   a. red

   b. green

   c. purple

   d. blue

23 A series of linked pages which you have been following is often referred to as a

   a. network

   b. web

   c. strand

   d. thread

24 Which of the following is NOT an option in the Find dialog box used to locate text in a Web page?

   a. start

   b. Find Next

   c. Match case

   d. Direction

25 Newest items added to the Bookmark list will appear

   a. at the top of the list

   b. at the bottom of the list

   c. alphabetically within the existing list

   d. under the heading, New Entries, at the end of the existing bookmark list

APPLICATIONS
REVIEW

1 Find, start, and stop links.

   a. Start Netscape.

   b. Scroll down and click the link WWW Illustrated Online Companion on your home page.

   c. Find and click the link Exploring business under the heading Exploring the Web.

   d. Before the page finishes loading, click the Stop button on the toolbar.

   e. Click the Reload button on the toolbar to finish loading the page.

2 Jump backward and forward.

   a. Click the Back button on the toolbar to return to the WWW Illustrated Online Companion.

   b. Click the Forward button on the toolbar to see the Exploring business page.

   c. Continue to select the Back button until it dims.

   d. Select the Forward button to display the next page.

   e. Choose a link from the page. Once the new page loads, use the Back and Forward buttons to locate the WWW Illustrated Online Companion page.

3 Go home.

   a. Click the Home button on the tool bar.

   b. Click the WWW Illustrated Online Companion on the home page.

   c. Select a link from the companion. Wait for the page to finish loading.

   d. Press [Alt][G][H] to return home.

   e. Click the Back button twice, then click the Home button.

4 View history.

   a. Click the View History command on the Go menu.

   b. Find and select WWW Illustrated Online Companion in the list box.

   c. Click the Go To button in the dialog box.

   d. Click the Close button in the dialog box.

   e. Click the Home button.

   f. Use the History command to return to the page you previously loaded.

5 Find text.

   a. Click the Home button on the toolbar.

   b. Click the Find button on the toolbar.

   c. Type "Web" in the Find What text box.

   d. Locate all the occurrences of the word "Web" in your home page.

   e. Close the Find dialog box.

6 Use Bookmarks.

   a. Click the Add Bookmark command on the Bookmarks menu.

   b. Load the WWW Illustrated Online Companion.

   c. Add the current page to your bookmark list.

   d. Find and select the link Exploring Electronic Publishing under the heading Exploring the Web.

   e. Select the View Bookmarks command on the Bookmarks menu.

   f. Use the Bookmark List to return to WWW Illustrated Online Companion.

   g. Return to the Electronic Publishing page and add it to your bookmark list.

   h. If you're working in a lab, remove the bookmarks you added to your bookmark list.

7 Enter a URL address.

   a. Click the Open button on the toolbar.

   b. In the Open Location text box, type "http://www.ibm.com/".

   c. Click Open.

   d. Explore this Web site using the techniques and tools you learned about in this unit.

   e. Click the Home button when you are done, and exit Netscape.

INDEPENDENT
CHALLENGE 1

You are the administrative assistant to John Prescott, the president of Words and Wisdom, a small promotional company that specializes in writing ads, promotional pieces, and jingles. John travels a great deal promoting his company's services. He wants to trade in his desktop computer for a laptop he can take with him on his business trips. He has narrowed the search down to five computer makers, and he asks you to investigate their offerings using the Web. These are the computer firm's URLs:

http://www.compaq.com/

http://www.ibm.com/

http://www.apple.com/

http://www.hp.com/

http://www.nec.com/

Use Netscape to research what information is available on the Web concerning these firms, and print a page from the site of the firm you think offers the most attractive laptop computer line.

INDEPENDENT
CHALLENGE 2

You recently landed a job as a columnist for a popular computer magazine. One of your responsibilities will be to write a monthly column called Tech Update, which will chronicle the latest developments in software and hardware technology. Add the following Web sites to your Bookmark List so you can browse them for information that will help you stay abreast of what the major players in the technology industry are doing.

http://www.compaq.com/

http://www.ibm.com/

http://www.apple.com/

http://www.hp.com/

Once you store the initial pages of these sites in the Bookmark List, use the list to revisit the initial page for each site and investigate the company's offerings. Print a page of the site that most impresses you, and then remove all four sites from the Bookmark List.

INDEPENDENT
CHALLENGE 3

In a few months, you will be graduating from college with a teaching degree. You have been examining the job market and are feeling quite discouraged. A friend suggests you look into the Peace Corps, and you decide to look into the organization and see what it is all about. You remember that AT&T has put its 800-number directories on the Web. Use the following URL to look up the 800 number for the Peace Corps, located in Washington, D.C.

http://att.net/dir800

After you locate the 800 phone number, print a copy of the page containing the number.

INDEPENDENT
CHALLENGE 4

Your parents have decided to buy a computer for the family to use. Your parents want to buy a Macintosh computer, but you are used to using a computer running Windows, and you want to convince your parents that Windows is the way to go. A classmate gives you a URL that is supposed to provide information on all types of personal computers. Enter the following URL and investigate the kinds of information available at this site on Microsoft Windows.

http://ici.proper.com/

Print the most interesting page you find on computers equipped to run Windows to show to your parents.

Searching
THE WEB

In the last unit, you learned how to navigate the World Wide Web using Netscape. However, the Web is an enormous network, and simply navigating from one page to the next is a very slow and inefficient way to find information on a specific subject. Fortunately, there are a number of search tools on the Web to help you quickly locate what you want. The major ones are **subject-oriented catalogs** (lists arranged from A to Z), **guides** (new, outstanding, and unusual Web pages), **maps** (locations of Web sites displayed geographically), and **spiders** (indices of Web page contents). ► In this unit, you will learn how to use these search tools effectively and efficiently to locate information for The Nut Tree's on-line marketing effort. ►

Understanding search methods

There are four basic search techniques to find information on the Web: (1) by subject, (2) by guide, (3) by location, and (4) by content. Table 3-1 indicates strategies for finding information with each of these search techniques. This table also provides a list of the available search tools for use with each search technique.

▶ Note that a **subject-oriented search** works well to find general or broad information (e.g., an overview of the commercial services on the Web). A **guide-oriented search** is most appropriate when you want to locate new, outstanding, or unusual pages (e.g., a guide to cool pages on the Web). A **location-oriented search** works well when you are looking for sites in a specific geographical area (e.g., commercial Web sites in Milwaukee). Finally, a **content-oriented search** is best for pinpointing links to Web pages covering a specific topic (e.g., advertising agencies on the Web). See Figure 3-1 for examples of the four most common methods for searching the Web. Because information on the Web is not always well organized or accurate (see related topic "Warning about Web information"), an integrated approach to searching the Web gives you the best chance of finding the resources you want. Use the following integrated strategies or guidelines to minimize your search time and maximize search results.

- Search broadly at first to determine the breadth of information available on the subject

- Look for pages with collections of links to the subject

- Find new, outstanding, and unusual Web pages on the subject

- Locate sites related to the subject

- Search narrowly to find Web pages, titles, and URLs that contain a specific topic

- Navigate all the links you find to identify additional resources on the subject (this activity is often referred to as **surfing the Web**)

FIGURE 3-1: Four common search methods

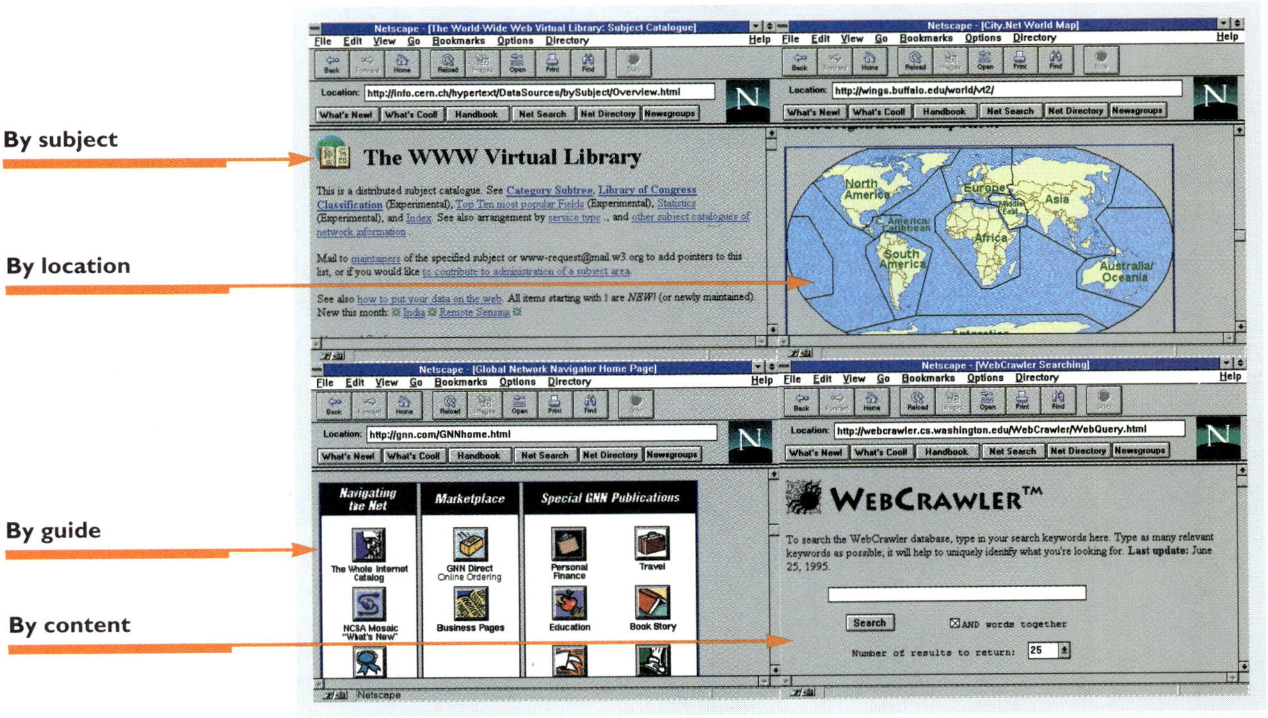

By subject

By location

By guide

By content

Warning about Web information

Information on the Web is typically entered and maintained by volunteers. Thus, this data is not always reliable or well organized. Be skeptical of what you find on the Web, and always attempt to verify its completeness and accuracy with other sources. Also, try to look for reputable sources that are well known (e.g., Harvard Business School).

TABLE 3-1: Strategies for searching the Web

TO FIND	EXAMPLE	SEARCH BY	TOOLS
General information	Overview of electronic publishing on the Web	Subject	Subject-oriented catalogs (e.g., The WWW Virtual Library, Yahoo, and Planet Earth)
The new, cool, and unusual	New company home pages	Guide	Travel or tour guides (e.g., Spry City, Global Network Navigator, and Edge of the Web)
A particular Web site	Commercial Web sites in Milwaukee, WI	Location	Maps (e.g., the Virtual Tourist) and directories of sites organized by location (e.g., the Wanderer)
A specific topic	Web server software	Content	Spiders (e.g., the WebCrawler and Jumpstation)

Searching by subject

If you are unsure of where to start investigating a subject, or you want a quick overview of the subject, begin your search with a subject-oriented catalog. A subject-oriented catalog is just a list of topics arranged alphabetically to facilitate browsing. Typically, you will find subtopics indented under each major heading in the catalog, as shown in Figure 3-2. This hierarchical organization, or hierarchical tree, lets you quickly browse the available subjects and their subtopics.

▶ Melissa Shea, owner of The Nut Tree, asks you to find out more about what commercial services exist on the Web to help the company establish an on-line presence. You can use The WWW Virtual Library to determine what types of business services are available via the Web.

1 Start Netscape and click the **WWW Illustrated Online Companion** link on your home page
The WWW Illustrated Online Companion page appears in your document window.

2 Scroll down to find and click the **Search by subject** link
A page with links to subject-oriented search sites appears in your document window.

3 Click **The WWW Virtual Library** link
The WWW Virtual Library overview page appears, as shown in Figure 3-3.

4 Find and click the **Category Subtree** link
The subject-oriented catalog appears, as shown in Figure 3-4.

5 Scroll down to find and click the **Commercial Services** link
A Yellow Pages listing of commercial services on the Internet appears in your document window.

6 Scroll down the list and examine the available topics

7 Click the **Home button** on the toolbar
Your home page reappears in the document window.

FIGURE 3-2:
Alphabetical and
hierarchical structure
of a subject-oriented
catalog

Major subject heading

Subtopic

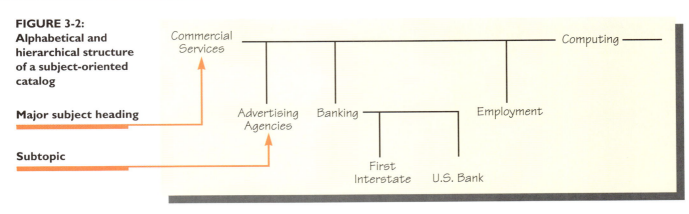

FIGURE 3-3: The WWW Virtual Library overview page

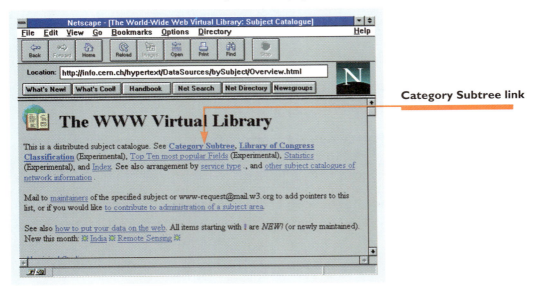

Category Subtree link

FIGURE 3-4: The WWW Virtual Library subject-oriented catalog

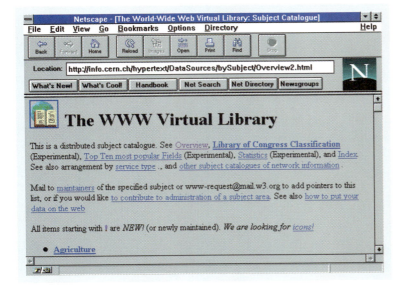

TROUBLE?
If you are unable to connect to The WWW Virtual Library (i.e., if you receive an error message or the page fails to load after a long time), select another subject-oriented search tool from the Search the Web section of the WWW Illustrated Online Companion page to complete this lesson.■

Searching by guide

There are tens of thousands of Web sites and, even more astonishing, the number of sites continues to double about every two months. In order to organize these resources and make them readily available to Web users, individuals and organizations on the Web have created **guides**, which are navigational aids that list and describe interesting and useful sites. Guides are often a terrific resource for finding more information on a subject, especially new, cool, and unusual Web pages. ▶ Intrigued by what you have found so far, you decide to use a guide to help you find some of the better commercial resources on the Web.

STEPS

1 Click the **WWW Illustrated Online Companion** link on your home page
   The WWW Illustrated Online Companion page appears.

2 Click the **Search by guide** link
   A page with links to directory and guide pages appears.

3 Click the **Global Network Navigator (GNN)** link and scroll down the page to display the **Marketplace icons**
   A list of icons like those shown in Figure 3-5 appears.

4 Click the **Business Pages icon** and scroll down to the Alphabetical List
   The document window changes to display the alphabetical listing of the GNN Business Pages, as shown in Figure 3-6.

5 Click the **Business Services** link
   The GNN Business Pages home page appears, as shown in Figure 3-7.

6 Click the **Home button** 🏠
   Your home page reappears in the document window.

FIGURE 3-5:
Spry City page

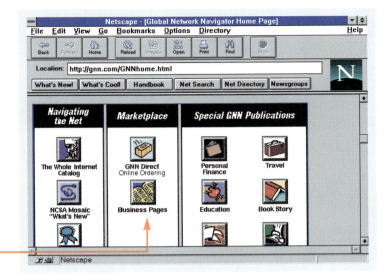

Business Pages icon

FIGURE 3-6:
Spry City Business
Center

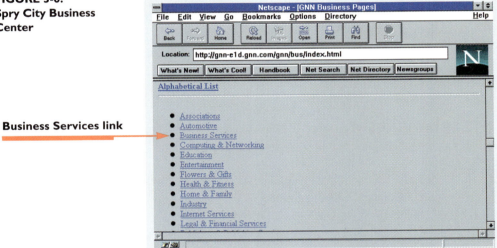

Business Services link

FIGURE 3-7:
Outstanding Business
Information and
Resources

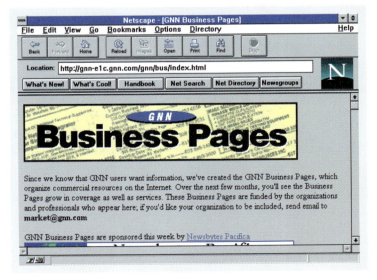

QUICK **TIP**

The What's New!
button on the
Netscape directory
button bar takes you
to a list of sites
recently added to the
Web. The What's
Cool! button displays
a guide to sites of out-
standing quality and
content. To see
unusual Web pages,
visit the Edge of the
Web using the Search
by guide link located
on your WWW
Illustrated Online
Companion page.■

TROUBLE?

If the hypertext links
described in the
lessons have changed,
look around for other
business resources.■

Searching by location

When you want to see what Web sites are available in a certain geographical area, maps provide an excellent way to get a bird's-eye view. **Web maps** are special images that depict the geography of an area. They include labeled areas (hyper-regions) you can select for closer examination. ▶ For example, a typical location-oriented search begins with a map of the world. You start by clicking the region you want to investigate (e.g., North America). A second map appears, showing the countries in the area. After choosing a country (e.g., the United States), you may be presented with additional maps to narrow your search further. Eventually, you will work your way down to a collection of Web sites for the area you are interested in (e.g., Seattle, Washington). ▶ You would like to see what commercial Web services are available in your local area. The Nut Tree is located in Seattle. You can use Web maps to find a collection of sites to call or visit personally.

1 Click the **WWW Illustrated Online Companion** link on your home page
The WWW Illustrated Online Companion page appears in the document window.

2 Click the **Search by location** link
The Search by location page appears.

3 Click the **Virtual Tourist II** link
After some time, the Virtual Tourist home page appears in your document window.

4 Scroll down the page to display the world map, as shown in Figure 3-8, and click the **North America** hyperregion
A second Virtual Tourist page appears in your document window.

5 Scroll down to see the country map, as illustrated in Figure 3-9, and click the **United States** hyperregion
A third Virtual Tourist map page appears.

6 Scroll down to see the map of states, as shown in Figure 3-10, and click **WA**
A listing of cities for Washington state appears.

7 Click **Seattle** and look for commercial services or sites in the local area
If you are unable to find any commercial resources in the area, return to the Seattle page; then select a different link and try again.

8 Once you are done exploring, click the **Home button**
Your home page appears in the document window.

FIGURE 3-8: Virtual Tourist world map

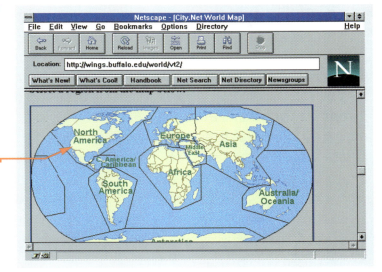

North America hyperregion

FIGURE 3-9: Virtual Tourist country map

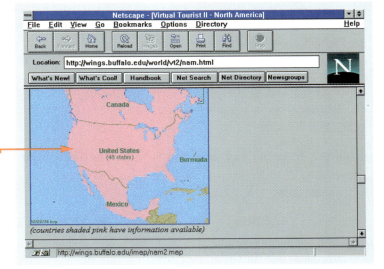

United States hyperregion

FIGURE 3-10: Virtual Tourist state map

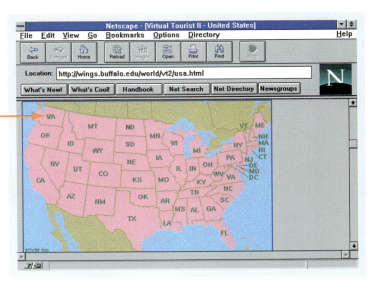

Washington state hyperregion

QUICK **TIP**

You can also find Web resources by geographical area with lists. If you know the name of the site you want to find, you can use a directory of Web sites organized by location to search for it. For example, **The Wanderer** offers Web sites arranged under geographical headings. However, this text-based search method doesn't provide the same geographical overview, or "lay of the land," that maps offer.■

TROUBLE?

If the Virtual Tourist is unavailable, use another location-oriented search tool from the Search by location page to find commercial resources in Seattle, Washington.■

Searching by content

When you want to find information on a specific topic, your best bet is to use a spider. A **spider** is a program that travels the Web to gather, compile, and index information, so it can later locate Web pages based on their content. A spider uses a **search form**, a Web page that lets you specify the information to search for using **key word(s)** that represent your topic of interest. The actual search process is conducted by a **search engine**, a program that uses the entries in the search form to scan for relevant information stored in an index. ► Impressed by the commercial services you have discovered, you now decide to find a list of agencies that specialize in on-line advertising. Since you have a specific topic you want to find, "advertising agencies," the most expedient way to conduct the search is with a spider.

1   Click the **WWW Illustrated Online Companion** link on your home page, then once the WWW Illustrated Online Companion page opens, click the **Search by content** link
A page with links to spiders appears.

2   Click **WebCrawler**
The Search the Web form appears, as shown in Figure 3-11. Table 3-2 describes the options available in this search form.

3   Click the **search text box** and type **advertising agencies**
The words appear in the search text box. Note that neither word is capitalized. It is unnecessary in this search to worry about capitalization.

4   Make sure the **AND words together check box** is selected to ensure that the search engine looks for Web pages that are relevant to "advertising agencies," not just "advertising" or "agencies"

5   If necessary, scroll down to the **Number of results to return list box**
The larger the number of requested responses, the longer the search process will take.

6   To reduce search time, click the **down arrow** in the **Number of results to return list box**, then click **10** on the drop-down list
WebCrawler will now limit this search to 10 results.

7   Click the **Search button**
After some time, WebCrawler's search results appear in your document window like those shown in Figure 3-12. The numbers to the left of the results are a relevancy index that indicates how closely the results matched the search (1000 represents a perfect match).

8   Click the first link on the list, explore the sight, then click the **Home button** 🏠 and exit Netscape

FIGURE 3-11:
Search the Web
form

Number of results to
return list box

Search text box

Search button

AND words together
check box

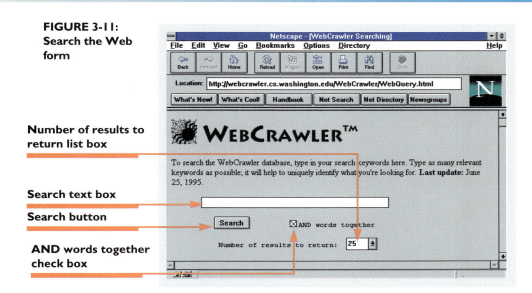

QUICK TIP

In some searches
capitalization is impor-
tant. For example,
when searching for
proper names like
George Washington,
correct capitalization
is critical to finding
what you want. ■

QUICK TIP

Although search
engines may be used
by search tools other
than spiders, the
information they
return varies greatly.
The information
search engines find is
based on things like
document titles and
URL names, not the
actual text within
Web pages. ■

FIGURE 3-12:
WebCrawler search
results

Number of results
returned

Number of documents
found by query

Relevancy index

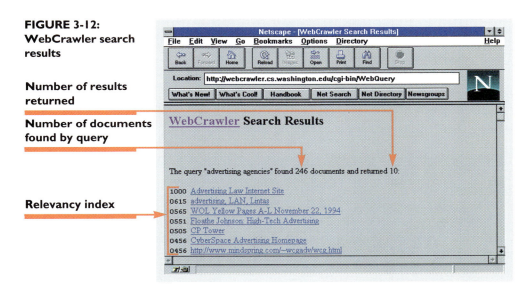

TABLE 3-2: Options in the Searching the Web form

OPTION	DESCRIPTION
Search text box	Allows the entry of key word(s) to search for
Search button	Starts the searching process
AND words together check box	If checked, it causes the search engine to look for topics that include *all* key words entered in the search text box. If unchecked, the search engine will look for topics that include *any* of the key words entered in the search text box.
Number of results to return list box	Limits how many responses the search engine will return

TASKREFERENCE

TASK	METHOD	TOOLS
Search for general information	Subject search	Catalogs
Search for the new, cool, and unusual	Guide search	Travel or tour guides
Search for a specific Web site	Site/location search	Maps, directories of sites
Search for a specific topic	Content search	Spiders

CONCEPTSREVIEW

Briefly describe the four indicated elements of the WebCrawler search form shown in Figure 3-13.

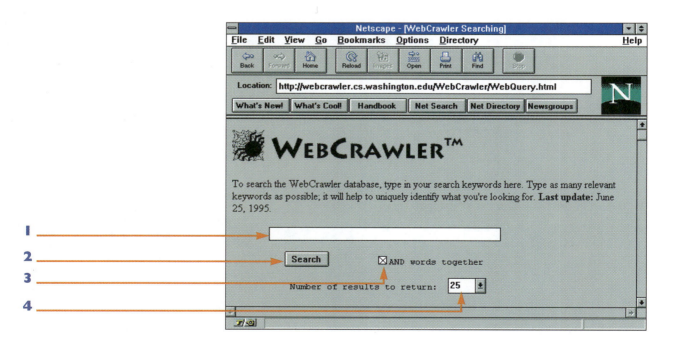

FIGURE 3-13

Match each term with the statement that best describes its function.

5 The WWW Virtual Library

6 Search button

7 Global Network Navigator (GNN)

8 Virtual Tourist

9 Hyperregions

   a. Location-oriented search site

   b. Guide site

   c. Areas in an image you can select

   d. Subject-oriented search catalog

   e. Starts the search process

Select the best answer from the list of choices.

10 Which of the following are *not* search tools?

   a. Maps

   b. Spiders

   c. Cards

   d. Guides

11 Which of the following is *not* a search strategy?

   a. Search generally at first

   b. Search for rare occurrences

   c. Locate related sites by surfing the Web

   d. Narrow your search with content-based spiders

12 The WWW Virtual Library is

   a. An owner-oriented search tool

   b. A location-oriented search tool

   c. A content-oriented search tool

   d. A subject-oriented search tool

13 Global Network Navigator lets you search by

   a. Location

   b. Guide

   c. Spider

   d. Subject

14 The WebCrawler lets you search by

   a. Content

   b. Location

   c. Subject

   d. Guide

15 The Virtual Tourist lets you search by

   a. Guide

   b. Index

   c. Password

   d. Location

16 The Number of results to return list box in the WebCrawler search form lets you

   a. Limit the number of terms

   b. Restrict the number of keywords

   c. Limit a certain number of results to be reported

   d. Limit the number of capitalized words displayed

17 The search text box in the WebCrawler search form lets you

   a. Enter key words to save

   b. Select a subject title

   c. Enter key words to search on

   d. Choose another text box

18 A search engine is a program that lets you search for

   a. Everything on the Web

   b. Hierarchical Internet sites

   c. Information stored in an index

   d. Your history

APPLICATIONS
REVIEW

1 Search by subject.

a. Start Netscape and select <u>WWW Illustrated Online Companion</u> on your home page.

b. Select <u>Search by subject</u>.

c. Choose <u>The Whole Internet Catalog from O'Reilly and Associates</u> link.

d. Scroll down and select the <u>Business & Finance</u> link.

e. Explore (surf) some of the links on the page that appears.

f. Return to your home page.

2 Search by guide.

a. Select <u>WWW Illustrated Online Companion</u> on your home page.

b. Choose the <u>Search by guide</u> link.

c. Select the <u>Global Network Navigator (GNN)</u> link.

d. Scroll down the GNN home page and select the Best of the Net icon in the Navigating the Net section.

e. Explore a selection from the Best of the Net list.

f. Return to your home page.

3 Search by location.

a. Select <u>WWW Illustrated Online Companion</u> on your home page.

b. Choose <u>Search by location</u>.

c. Select Virtual Tourist II.

d. Scroll down to the map of the world and select the <u>Asia</u> region.

e. Scroll down to the country map and choose <u>R.O.C. Taiwan</u>.

f. Scroll down to the Maps heading and select the <u>Interactive Map of Taiwan</u> link.

g. Once the map loads, click the topmost box on the map to see Taipei.

h. When you finish exploring Taiwan, return to your home page.

4 Search by location.

a. Select <u>WWW Illustrated Online Companion</u> on your home page.

b. Choose <u>Search by location</u>.

c. Select <u>The Wanderer</u>.

d. When the Comprehensive List of Sites appears, scroll down the page to display the Domains list box.

e. Use the scroll down arrow at the right edge of the Domains list box to scroll down to eg -Egypt, then click the Submit Query button.

f. Select one of the links listed for Egypt and explore the site.

g. When you finish exploring, return to your home page.

5 Search by content.

a. Select <u>WWW Illustrated Online Companion</u> on your home page.

b. Choose <u>Search by content</u>.

c. Select <u>Jumpstation</u>.

d. Choose <u>The Document Search</u> link.

e. When the next page loads, read the instructions for using this search engine, then select <u>The Document Search</u> link.

f. Click the Enter subject word text box and type "server software."

g. Click the Submit button.

h. When the search results appear, scroll down the list and explore links to Web server software.

i. Return to your home page.

INDEPENDENT
CHALLENGE 1

As you begin your first week as the columnist for Tech Update, familiarize yourself with the current issues in computing and technology. Access The WWW Virtual Library to find out what subtopics are listed under the subject heading "Computing." Explore three of these subtopics, and write a separate paragraph summarizing each subtopic to bring to the magazine's next issue-planning meeting scheduled for later in the week.

INDEPENDENT
CHALLENGE 2

A recent article you read mentioned that a lot of people are finding jobs using the Web. Load the Spry Home Page, select the More of the Best icon, and then choose the link to Business. Explore one of the listings under the heading Job Hunting. (For an example of a job hunting resource, see Figure 3-14.) Print a copy of the more interesting positions you find advertised there.

FIGURE 3-14: Monster Board

INDEPENDENT
CHALLENGE 3

After speaking with a Peace Corps representative and reviewing the large packet of information they mailed to you, you discover there are several teaching positions open in South Africa for which you would be eligible. However, you know very little about this country. Use the Virtual Tourist maps to find

1 what types of food are eaten in South Africa,

2 what the climate is like, and

3 what the size of the population of South Africa is.

INDEPENDENT
CHALLENGE 4

John Prescott, your boss at Words and Wisdom, was very pleased with how well you utilized the World Wide Web to help him make an informed choice for a laptop computer. He now suggests you use the Web to find information that would be helpful in solving some of the company's other computing needs. For example, he is interested in purchasing server software. Find some on-line sources that sell server software. You can use a spider to find several "virtual" outlets that sell server software. Print a copy of the sites you find. Your printout should look similar to the one shown in Figure 3-15.

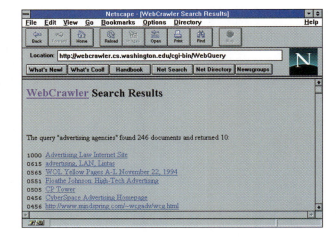

FIGURE 3-15: List of sites offering server software

UNIT 4

Exploring
THE WEB

N ow that you know how to navigate and search the World Wide Web, it's time to explore some of the major categories of activity on the Web. In this unit, you'll take a look at the areas of business, education, electronic publishing, entertainment, government, and home pages. You'll visit shopping malls, universities, museums, government sites, and personal home pages. ▶ As on-line marketing manager for The Nut Tree, you need to know more about the interests and desires of your potential customers so that you can better design a company home page that appeals to Web users. You decide to explore some of the major areas of interest on the Web to see what types of sites and information are attracting Web users. You may find some useful information for your marketing efforts as well. ▶

Understanding categories of information on the Web

Understanding how the information on the Web is organized is useful because it makes it easier to locate the information of interest to you. Also, it helps the people who access and exchange information on the Web to do so more efficiently. The immense traffic on the Web is managed by dividing the information available on the Web into categories. Typical categories include business, education, electronic publishing, entertainment, government, research, science, technology, and so forth. The following bulleted list contains six of the more popular categories of interest on the Web, as shown in Figure 4-1. Each of the major categories is divided into separate subtopics. ▶ This list is not intended to be a comprehensive representation of what's on the Web. Instead, the focus here is on the types of sites that people visit, and visit often. In other words, this classification scheme is meant to help you identify the high traffic areas of the Web. For more information on Web usage, see the related topic "Who is using the Web?" in this lesson. ▶ This information will be particularly useful as you determine how to design The Nut Tree home page so as to attract Web users.

- **Business**—employment, investing, and shopping

- **Education**—schools on the Web and on-line libraries

- **Electronic publishing**—electronic books, magazines (e-zines), and newspapers

- **Entertainment**—art galleries and museums, movies, TV, and travel

- **Government**—branch, department, independent establishment, or government agency

- **Home pages**—organizations and personal

FIGURE 4-1: Categories of information on the Web

Six popular categories of information

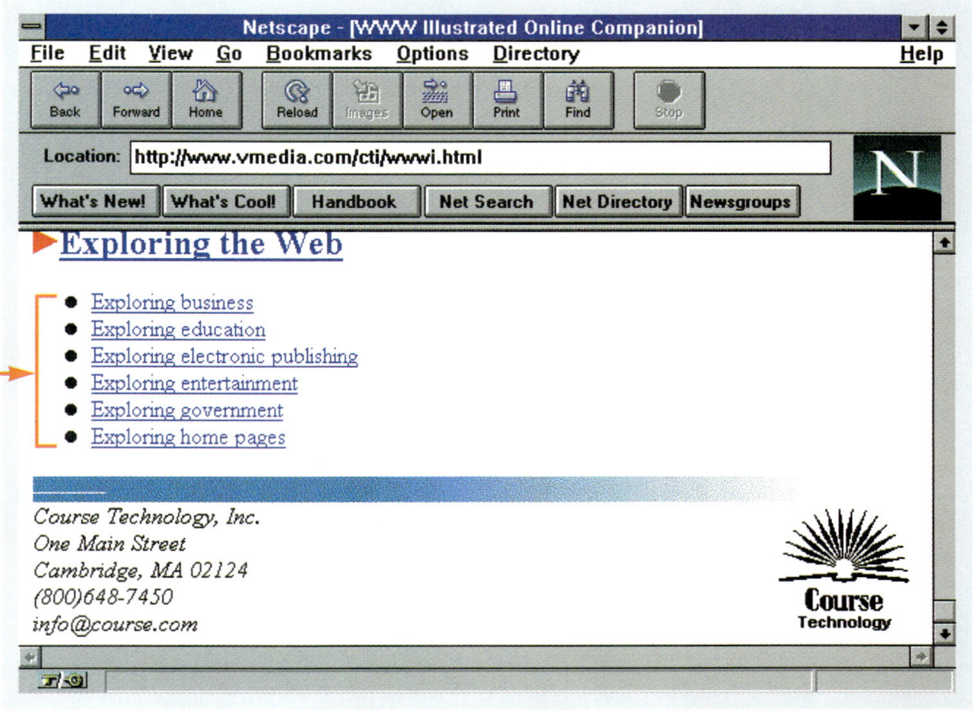

Who is using the Web?

Currently, the number of Web users is estimated to be in the range of 1 to 1.5 million. The majority of users are between the ages 18 and 34 years old. However, because the speed and availability of the Web is expected to improve quickly, most marketing projections indicate that by 1999 there will be over 40 million Web users, including a much wider range in ages.

Exploring business

The business category represents the fastest growing segment of the Web. Employment, investing, and shopping top the list of business areas that interest Web users. Shopping is a particularly popular activity. ▶ The Web has an impressive collection of **virtual shopping malls**, which are groups of **on-line storefronts** or **cybershops** where companies market their goods and services on the World Wide Web. Just like real malls, virtual malls have their upsides and downsides. ▶ For example, a popular virtual mall can greatly increase the number of people who view your home page; however, there will typically be a higher fee for membership in a well-known mall (similar to the fee for leasing space in a real mall). See the related topic "Virtual storefronts" in this lesson to learn how large companies have avoided setting up shop in a virtual mall. ▶ You decide to visit the Internet Mall, one of the larger and better-known virtual shopping malls, to tour specialty food shops like The Nut Tree.

1. Start Netscape and click the link **WWW Illustrated Online Companion** on your home page

2. Click the **Exploring business** link under the **Exploring the Web** heading
   The page listing links to business resources appears in your document window.

3. Scroll down the page until you see the list of links to shopping malls, then click the link **Internet Mall**
   After a brief period, The Internet Mall home page appears, similar to those shown in Figure 4-2. The Internet Mall has over 1000 cybershops, ranging from food suppliers to travel agents. The Food and Beverages link looks promising for finding specialty snack shops like The Nut Tree.

4. Click the **Food and Beverages** link
   The document window changes to display a page like the one shown in Figure 4-3. The Sweets and Snacks link seems the mostly likely candidate to lead to shops selling products like yours.

5. Click the **Sweets and Snacks** link
   A page listing cybershops appears.

6. Scroll down the page and select a cybershop to visit, such as Sophisticated Chocolates
   The home page for the company appears. For example, the Sophisticated Chocolates home page offers gift boxes and baskets, chocolate corporate logos, and custom favors for weddings and other events.

7. When you have finished, click the **Home button** on the toolbar
   Your home page reappears in the document window.

FIGURE 4-2: Internet Mall

FIGURE 4-3: Food and Beverages categories

**Sweets and
Snacks link**

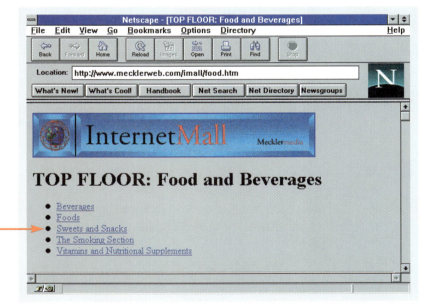

Virtual storefronts

Many large corporations do not need to rely on the marketing presence of a virtual mall to ensure high-volume use of their home pages. Instead, they choose to create their own **virtual storefront**, or Web site, to establish a unique and individual presence on the Web. For example, Pizza Hut, Microsoft, Digital Equipment, and IBM have their own individual sites on the Web. These large and well-known corporations have a wealth of resources and the drawing power to attract Web users all by themselves.

TROUBLE?

Some virtual malls have security systems. If a dialog box appears stating that the mall or storefront you have selected is secured, click OK and continue.■

Exploring education

Educational institutions have been active in the Internet community for decades. Not surprisingly, some of the most impressive Web sites are located at colleges and universities around the world. For more information on educational Web sites, see the related topic "Why schools are interested in the Web." Also, on-line libraries have recently been attracting quite a bit of attention. This is because **on-line libraries** provide publications in an electronic form easily accessible to Web users. ▶ You are considering returning to school to complete a master's degree in business administration to improve your effectiveness as the marketing manager of The Nut Tree. You can use the Web to explore business programs that might interest you.

1 Click **WWW Illustrated Online Companion** on your home page

2 Click the **Exploring education** link under the **Exploring the Web** heading
   The page listing links to educational resources appears in your document window.

3 Click **BSCHOOLWeb: Marr's Official Rating Guide To Business School Webs**
   The home page for the BSCHOOLWeb: Marr's Official Rating Guide To Business School Webs appears, as shown in Figure 4-4. This guide contains pointers, descriptions, and ratings of the home pages of business schools around the world.

4 Select the link to the top-rated business school home pages
   The document window changes to display the top-rated business school sites, similar to the one shown in Figure 4-5.

5 Scroll down and click a site, such as **Stanford Graduate School of Business**
   The home page for the business school you select appears in the document window. For example, the Stanford Graduate School of Business home page is one of the best business school sites on the Web.

6 Search the page for information on MBA programs; if a link exists, click it to see information on the program

7 When you finish, click the **Home button** [Home] to return to your home page

FIGURE 4-4: BSCHOOLWeb: Marr's Official Rating Guide To Business School Webs

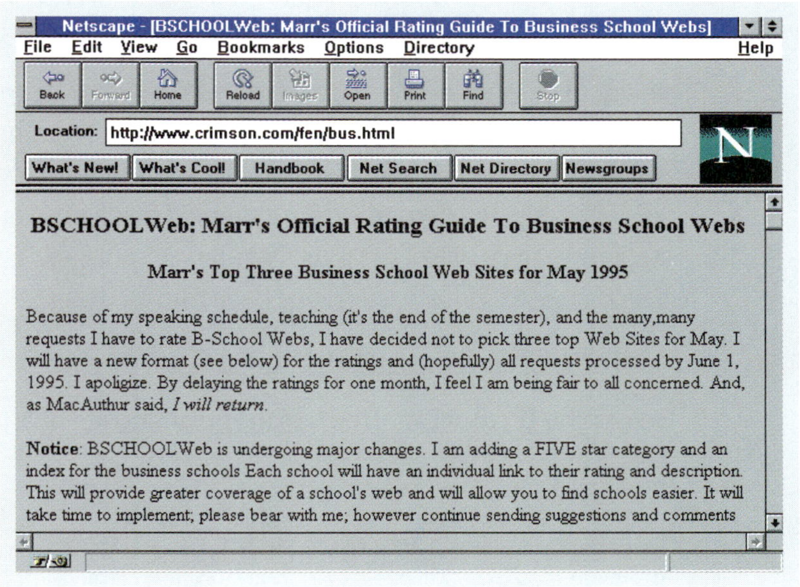

FIGURE 4-5: The BSCHOOLWeb: Top-rated business school page

Bulleted top-rated business school home page

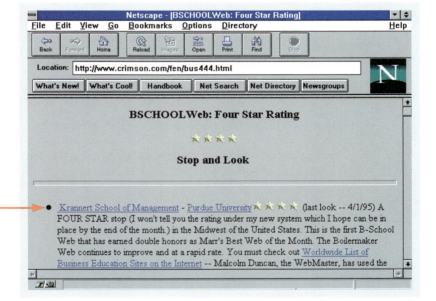

Why schools are interested in the Web

The World Wide Web offers a friendly and rich source of information for academic research. It is also a wonderful medium for improving communication between instructors and students. Faculty are finding the Web useful for providing up-to-date course materials such as syllabi and assignments to students. There are even entire courses being taught using the Web. The interactive nature of the Web makes it a very useful and attractive means of enhancing classroom instruction. Students really appreciate the ability to control the pace and direction of the learning process.

Exploring electronic publishing

The number of electronic publishers on the Web is exploding. New electronic books, magazines (e-zines), and newspapers appear almost daily. E-zines are the most popular because they typically use plenty of stunning images along with brief articles. ▶ Since the early Web users tended to be technically oriented, technology-related e-zines are currently the most well developed and impressive pages on the Web. Investigate one of the more popular computer e-zines on the Web to gain a better appreciation of what can be done with Web pages.

1   Click **<u>WWW Illustrated Online Companion</u>** on your home page

2   Select the **<u>Exploring electronic publishing</u>** link under the **<u>Exploring the Web</u>** heading

    A list of Web publishers appears.

3   Find and click the **<u>Ziff Davis Publishing</u>** link

    The ZD (Ziff Davis) net home page appears, like the one shown in Figure 4-6. This page contains links to Ziff Davis electronic publications. Many of these e-zines are interesting supplements to the company's paper-based magazines. (Remember that the Web is constantly changing, so don't worry if your document window displays new or different publications from those shown in the figure.)

4   Scroll down and click the **<u>PC MAGAZINE</u>** icon

    The home page for PC MAGAZINE on the Web appears, similar to the one shown in Figure 4-7. Notice the design of the page with its clean, crisp graphics.

5   Explore a link on this page that looks interesting to you

6   When you complete your explorations, click the **Home button** to return to your home page

FIGURE 4-6:
ZD Net home page

PC magazine icon

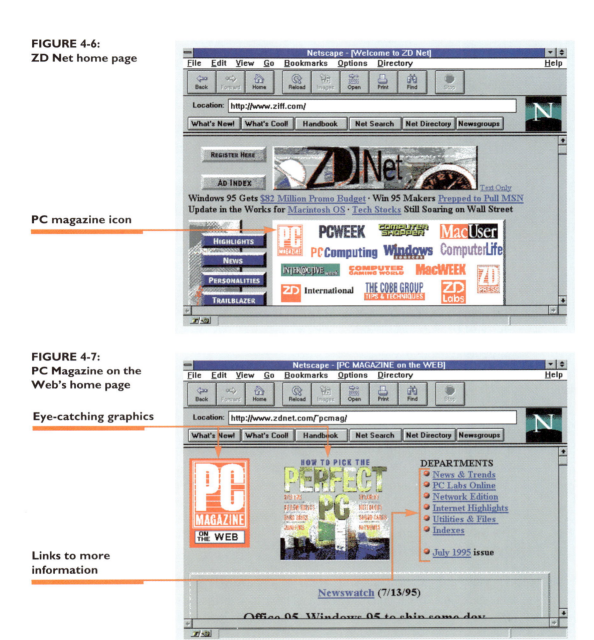

FIGURE 4-7:
PC Magazine on the Web's home page

Eye-catching graphics

Links to more information

QUICK TIP

For information on small business concerns, be sure to check out the Ideas DIGest ONLINE. This electronic magazine specializes in informative articles about small businesses.

Exploring entertainment

The interactive nature of the Web makes it a resource for all kinds of fun and entertainment. Chief among the entertainment areas on the Web are art galleries and museums, music, movies, TV, and travel. ▶ The graphical nature of the Web makes it a perfect way to provide colorful and interesting tours of digitized collections of artworks and exotic travel spots. The interactive nature of the Web also provides an easy way to locate and view information on movies, music, and TV. (If your computer is equipped with multimedia hardware and software, you can even listen to music or view video clips on the Web.) ▶ After viewing the graphics in e-zines in the previous lesson, you are convinced that the inclusion of graphics in The Nut Tree's Web page will make it much more effective in enticing customers. You realize, however, that some large graphics can really slow down the loading process. You have heard that some of the most striking images on the Web are digital representations of famous artworks hanging in galleries and museums around the world. Explore one of these sites to enjoy the view and see how they handle large image files.

1   Click **WWW Illustrated Online Companion** on your home page

2   Under the heading **Exploring the Web**, click the **Exploring Entertainment** link
The Exploring Entertainment Web page opens in the document window, listing links to art galleries and museums around the world. It is important to select a link that is geographically close to you; this can greatly reduce the time it takes to load large graphics.

3   Find and click the link closest to you geographically
The WebMuseum home page you selected appears in the document window, similar to the one shown in Figure 4-8.

4   To view a digitized representation of a painting, continue to make selections
After some time, an electronic image of a painting appears in your document window. For example, Figure 4-9 shows Renoir's famous painting *On the Terrace*.

5   When you are done appreciating the splendor of the paintings in the WebMuseum, click the **Home button**

FIGURE 4-8: WebMuseum home page

Netscape - [WebMuseum: Bienvenue! [Welcome from the curator]]

File   Edit   View   Go   Bookmarks   Options   Directory   Help

Back   Forward   Home   Reload   Images   Open   Print   Find   Stop

Location: http://www.oir.ucf.edu/louvre/

What's New!   What's Cool!   Handbook   Net Search   Net Directory   Newsgroups

LIKE A POOL   Japanese users: read all about the WebMuseum in an exclusive Like A Pool interview!

11 July 1995: Mark Harden invites you to discover Kasimir Malevich and **Suprematism.**

Bienvenue au WebMuseum!

As curator of this place, I would like to personally welcome you to a celebration of the WebMuseum million visitors from all over the world in just one year, with over 3 million documents

FIGURE 4-9: *On the Terrace* by Pierre-Auguste Renoir

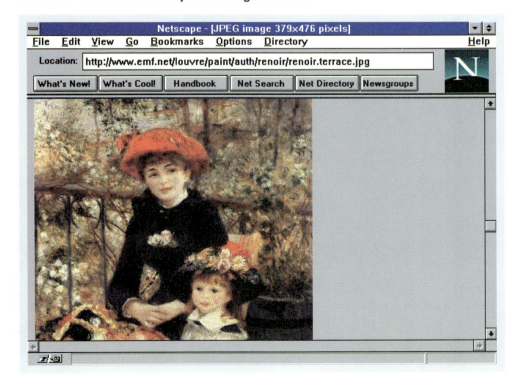

Netscape - [JPEG image 379x476 pixels]

File   Edit   View   Go   Bookmarks   Options   Directory   Help

Location: http://www.emf.net/louvre/paint/auth/renoir/renoir.terrace.jpg

What's New!   What's Cool!   Handbook   Net Search   Net Directory   Newsgroups

TROUBLE?

Loading and displaying large images of paintings and pictures can take a very long time. Be patient; it may take as long as 10 to 15 minutes for some images to finish loading. The actual length of loading time will vary depending on the size of the graphic chosen, the speed of your Internet connection, and the traffic on the Internet.■

Exploring government

The U.S. government is rushing to establish services on the Web at such a rate that it is sometimes hard to find the exact site you want. Fortunately, a one-stop shop exists to help you locate the federal site you are seeking. **FedWorld** is a subject-oriented catalog with links to hundreds of federal sites. See Table 4-1: Examples of federal resources on the Web. ▶ You want to explore what on-line help is available from government Web sites. You are especially interested in resources that will aid in expanding The Nut Tree's business into cyberspace and beyond the borders of the United States.

1 Click **WWW Illustrated Online Companion** on your home page

2 Click **Exploring government**
   A catalog of links to government sites on the Web appears in the document window.

3 Click the link **FedWorld** under the heading US Government Directories
   The home page for FedWorld appears, as shown in Figure 4-10.

4 Scroll down to the INDEX OF SUBJECT CATEGORIES heading, as shown in Figure 4-11

5 Click the **Behavior, Business, etc.** link
   A short time later, the document window displays the options for this category.

6 Click on one of the links, such as **Business, Commerce and Economics**
   A page of links appears (e.g., links to business, commerce and economics)

7 Click one of the federal sites listed on this page, such as **Small Business Administration**
   The home page for the chosen site appears, similar to the Small Business Administration (SBA) page shown in Figure 4-12.

8 Explore the site for resources that could help The Nut Tree in its growth (e.g., **Expanding Your Business**)

9 When you finish, click the **Home button** to return to your home page

TABLE 4-1: Examples of federal resources on the Web

TYPE OF FEDERAL SITE	EXAMPLES
Branch	1. Executive Branch (White House speeches); 2. Legislative Branch (Congressional bills); 3. Judicial Branch (Supreme Court decisions)
Department (Reports to the Executive Branch)	1. U.S. Department of Commerce (Information on international trade and commerce); 2. U.S. Department of Defense (Military-related information); 3. U.S. Department of Labor (Labor statistics)
Independent establishments and government agencies	1. Small Business Administration (SBA) (Small business related information); 2. Federal Bureau of Investigations (FBI) (The 10-most-wanted list and other criminal information); 3. U.S. Census Bureau (U.S. census data plus other statistical sources)

FIGURE 4-10:
FedWorld home page

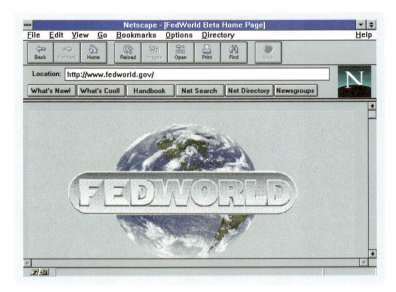

FIGURE 4-11:
FedWorld Index of
Subject Categories

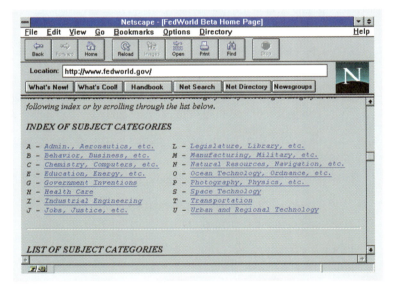

FIGURE 4-12:
Small Business
Administration (SBA)
home page

TROUBLE?

If you are unable
to connect to
FedWorld, select
another government
site under the
Exploring government
category in the
WWW Illustrated
Online Companion
(e.g., Small Business
Administration,
Department of
Commerce, etc.).■

Exploring home pages

The Web contains home pages for both organizations and individuals. Personal home pages are typically very innovative and fun to view. They can also be a great source of ideas for developing a unique and eye-catching company home page. Although no hard-and-fast rules exist for judging the quality of a home page, Table 4-2 does offer a list of characteristics that are common among the most popular home pages. Keep these characteristics in mind as you view different home pages on the Web. ▶ Melissa, now convinced that the Web represents a real business opportunity for The Nut Tree, asks you to design a home page for the company. As a first step, you'll visit a variety of home pages to gather innovative design ideas.

1 Click **WWW Illustrated Online Companion** on your home page

2 Click the **Exploring home pages** link under **Exploring the Web** heading

3 Click the **Who's Who on the Internet** link
The Who's Who on the Internet home page appears, as shown in Figure 4-13. This is a huge searchable directory of home pages arranged alphabetically.

4 To see the newest home pages added to the directory, click **review**
A list of recent additions to this directory appears.

5 Scroll down the list of home pages and click one, such as Mark Findlay's Home Page!
The selected home page appears in your document window, like the one shown in Figure 4-14.

6 When you finish your explorations, click the **Home button**  to return to your home page

7 Exit Netscape

TABLE 4-2: Characteristics of a good home page

HAVE	DON'T HAVE
• Innovative and eye-catching images	• Large images on the home page—bloated images slow loading and, thus, discourage visitors from returning
• Unique and valuable information	• Blatant advertisements
• Short and to-the-point Web pages	• Long, cluttered, or wordy pages
• Links to other related pages on the Web	• Nonfunctioning or outdated links
• Warning advising viewers of the size of files (e.g., still images, sound files, and video clips)	• Links to large files without labels or warnings about their size—users don't want to wait long periods to navigate your site
• Meaningful buttons and icons to help users quickly and easily find what they are looking for	• Obscure or hard-to-read icons

FIGURE 4-13: The Who's Who on the Internet home page

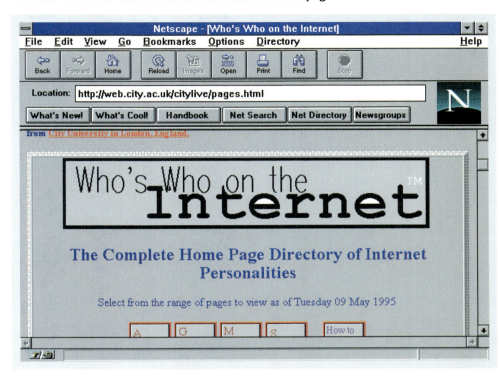

FIGURE 4-14: A personal home page

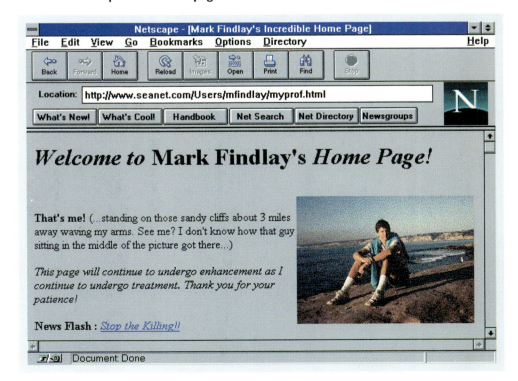

TASKREFERENCE

CATEGORIES OF WEB INFORMATION	SUBCATEGORIES	EXAMPLES
Business	Banking Investing Career services Shopping	Mortgage interest rates Daily stock market prices Average starting salary for public school teacher Purchase software
Education	On-line courses and schools Scholarships	Continuing education programs Available funding and how to apply
Electronic Publishing	Books Magazines (e-zines) Newspapers	On-line libraries Subscribe to magazine on cycling Read about political elections in France
Entertainment	Art galleries/museums Games Movies Music Travel Recreation	View the Mona Lisa in the Louvre Shareware video games Reviews of current films Tour schedules for performers Weather report for Bermuda Stats for favorite baseball team
Government	Branches Departments Independent establishments and government agencies	Information on Roe vs. Wade Terms on military enlistment EPA list of endangered species
Home Pages	Organizations and individuals	Course Technology's home page

CONCEPTSREVIEW

Visit and briefly describe the electronic publications indicated in Figure 4-15.

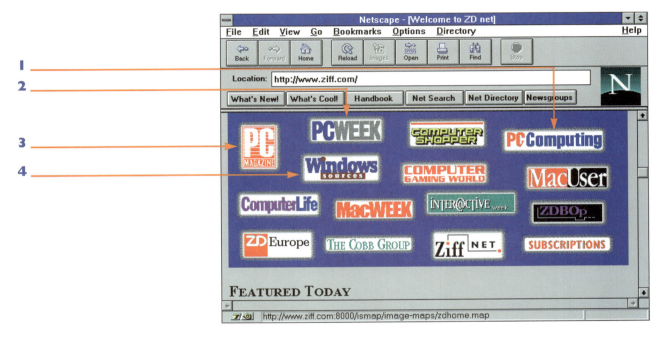

1
2

3

4

FIGURE 4-15

Match each of the terms below with the statement that best describes it function.

5 Virtual storefront

6 PC Magazine on the Web

7 U.S. federal agency

8 Virtual shopping mall

9 School on the Web

a. Electronic magazine

b. CIA

c. Harvard University

d. A place to shop on-line

e. On-line collection of places to shop

Select the best answer from the list of choices.

10 Which one of the following is *not* a business resource on the Web?

a. Banks

b. Investment sources

c. Myst

d. Virtual shopping malls

11 Which one of the following is *not* an entertainment area of interest on the Web?

a. Art galleries

b. Movies

c. TV

d. Interactive moon walks

12 A virtual shopping mall provides all of the following *except*

a. On-line advertising

b. A collection of company home pages

c. On-line purchasing

d. A place to meet other people

13 The following are all areas of interest for electronic publishing on the Web *except*

a. Electronic books

b. Electronic newspapers

c. E-zines

d. Electronic posters

14 Which of the following is *not* a federal government category?

a. Department

b. Office

c. Branch

d. Not for profit

15 Which of the following is *not* a characteristic of a good home page?

a. Short and concise

b. Large, impressive graphics

c. Links to related resources

d. Innovative and eye-catching images

16 The age range of Web users is

a. 16 to 25 years of age

b. 18 to 34 years of age

c. 20 to 35 years of age

d. 25 to 40 years of age

17 Which of the following is *not* a reason why a Web page may take a long time to load?

a. a large graphical image appears on the page

b. high traffic on the Internet

c. the speed of your connection to the Internet

d. the size of your computer monitor

18 FedWorld is

a. a subject-oriented catalog with links to hundreds of federal sites

b. a computer game

c. the Web site for the FBI

d. a government-produced e-zine on the state of the economy

19 Which Web category would you seek if you were planning to buy a house, and wanted to determine what a competitive mortgage interest rate would be?

a. home pages

b. electronic publishing

c. business

d. government

20 Which Web category would you seek if you were planning a trip to Europe, and you wanted to find out the best time of year to visit Switzerland?

a. entertainment

b. education

c. business

d. government

21 Which types of e-zines seem most popular today?

a. travel e-zines

b. business e-zines

c. entertainment e-zines

d. computer and technology e-zines

APPLICATIONS
REVIEW

1 Explore business.

  a. Start Netscape.

  b. Select the <u>WWW Illustrated Online Companion</u> on your home page.

  c. Choose the link <u>Exploring business</u>.

  d. Select the <u>Security Apl Quote Service</u> link under the Investing heading.

  e. When the Security Apl Quote Server page appears, scroll down to the <u>Ticker Symbol</u> text box and click it.

  f. To get stock quote information on the International Business Machines (IBM) Corporation, type "IBM" and click the Submit button.

  g. Review the search results.

  h. Use the search form on this page to retrieve a stock quote for MSFT (Microsoft Corporation).

  i. Return to your home page.

2 Explore education.

  a. Select the <u>WWW Illustrated Online Companion</u> on your home page.

  b. Click the link <u>Exploring education</u>.

  c. Choose the <u>Library of Congress</u> World Wide Web link under the heading Libraries on the Web.

  d. Select a topic from this page (e.g., <u>Exhibits and Events</u>).

  e. Explore one of the offerings on the topic you choose.

  f. Return to your home page.

3 Explore electronic publishing.

  a. Select the <u>WWW Illustrated Online Companion</u> on your home page.

  b. Click the link <u>Exploring electronic publishing</u>.

  c. Choose the <u>Mercury Center Web</u> link under the heading Electronic Newspapers.

  d. Find and read a news article on the Mercury Center Web page that interests you.

  e. Return to your home page.

4 Explore entertainment.

  a. Select the <u>WWW Illustrated Online Companion</u> on your home page.

  b. Click the link <u>Exploring entertainment</u>.

  c. Choose a link under the heading TV (e.g., <u>Lurker's Guide to Babylon V</u>).

  d. Investigate what is available at the site.

  e. If links to related sites exist (e.g., <u>Other Resources</u>), then explore one of them too.

  f. Return to your home page.

5 Explore government.

  a. Select the <u>WWW Illustrated Online Companion</u> on your home page.

  b. Click the link <u>Exploring government</u>.

  c. Choose one of the links under the heading Independent Establishments (e.g., <u>US Census bureau</u>).

  d. If available, find and read more information about the site (e.g., <u>About the Census Bureau</u>).

  e. Examine what the site has to offer.

  f. Return to your home page.

6 Explore home pages.

  a. Select the <u>WWW Illustrated Online Companion</u> and then <u>Exploring home pages</u>.

  b. Choose a link to personal home pages (e.g., <u>Home Pages of the Students, Faculty and Staff</u> at the University of Kansas).

  c. Explore the pages listed at the chosen site for unique and creative designs.

  d. Return to your home page.

7 Explore business.

  a. Select the <u>WWW Illustrated Online Companion</u> and then <u>Exploring business</u>.

  b. Pick a link under the Storefronts heading (e.g., <u>Pizza Hut</u>).

  c. Examine the home page for the chosen storefront.

  d. Return to the Exploring business home page and choose another storefront to investigate (e.g., <u>Adobe Systems, Inc.</u>).

  e. Return to your home page.

  f. Exit Netscape.

INDEPENDENT
CHALLENGE 1

The computer needs of a rapidly growing PR firm, Words and Wisdom, are becoming expensive. John Prescott realizes he will need to obtain additional funding to purchase state-of-the-art computers and peripherals for his new staff members. He asks you to find out about the business banking services available on the Web. To do this, you'll need to:

1 Select the WWW Illustrated Online Companion on your home page.

2 Click the link Exploring business.

3 Choose a link under the heading Banks on the Web (e.g., First Interstate Bank).

4 Find and read information about the on-line business-oriented banking services available from this institution (e.g., Business Services).

5 Print a copy of the most informative page you find.

INDEPENDENT
CHALLENGE 2

Your American history professor has assigned research topics for the final paper. Your paper is to be on the history of the White House. To gather more information about the executive branch of the federal government, do the following:

1 Select the WWW Illustrated Online Companion on your home page.

2 Click the link Exploring government.

3 Choose the link The White House under the Executive Branch heading.

4 Take one of the White House Tours, meet the The First Family, and sign the Guest Book.

5 Print a copy of the White House's home page to pass in with your research paper.

INDEPENDENT
CHALLENGE 3

You have applied and been accepted into the Peace Corps, and your first tour to South Africa begins next month. You need to get your financial affairs in order before you leave the country. Explore one of the money management and investment sites listed in the WWW Illustrated Online Companion (e.g., Fidelity Investments Information Center). Determine what resources are available to help you manage your money. Print a copy of the investment site's home page for future reference.

INDEPENDENT
CHALLENGE 4

An instructor wants to teach her students how to create their own home pages, and she is in search of an example of a page that has a good balance of text and clean graphics. Use the Exploring home pages link listed in the WWW Illustrated Online Companion to find and print two Web pages: a well-designed page and a page that could use some work. Make a list of how the second page could be improved upon. (Be sure to use the characteristics listed in Table 4-2.)

UNIT 5

▶ Plan a Web page

▶ Structure a Web page

▶ Save a file

▶ Write and format text

▶ Insert links to other Web pages

▶ Insert graphics

▶ View the page

▶ Test the links

Creating
A WEB PAGE

I n previous units you have explored the World Wide Web to view the information and resources available on it. You may have found yourself wondering how all these Web pages were created and placed on the Web. The process is actually quite straightforward, and the necessary tools are minimal. All you need to create a simple Web page is a word processor and a basic understanding of HTML, or HyperText Markup Language. **HTML** is the programming language used to describe the general structure of a Web page. HTML uses special characters, called **tags**, to enable your browser to properly display the contents of a Web page. ▶ Melissa wants you to create a sample home page for The Nut Tree. You'll use the mini word processor Notepad, included with Microsoft Windows 3.1, to create your Web page. ▶

Planning a Web page

As with any other kind of writing, it is important to approach the task of creating a Web page in a step-by-step manner. Otherwise, you are likely to end up with a complicated and poorly organized page. ► Although no hard-and-fast rules exist, the following steps will guide you in constructing a well-structured home page for The Nut Tree:

1   **Create an outline.**
The first step in creating a Web page is to write an outline. An outline for a home page should include a page title, an introductory paragraph, a list of links, an image (optional), and a contact address, as shown in Figure 5-1.

2   **Insert structuring tags for each element.**
Based on your outline, format the page by inserting HTML tags for each element of the page.

3   **Save the file.**
Copy the file to disk often to ensure against data loss.

4   **Write and format text.**
Enter the textual content of the page, adding any special formatting (e.g., boldface or italics).

5   **Insert links to other Web pages.**
Enter the hypertext links you want included on the page.

6   **Insert links to graphics.**
Enter the links to the images you want on the page.

7   **View the page.**
Examine the page with your Web browser to make sure it is structured correctly (e.g., see Figure 5-2). Make any necessary corrections to the page using your word processor.

8   **Test the hypertext links.**
Verify that the links on your page find and load the correct pages.

FIGURE 5-1: Sample outline for a Web page

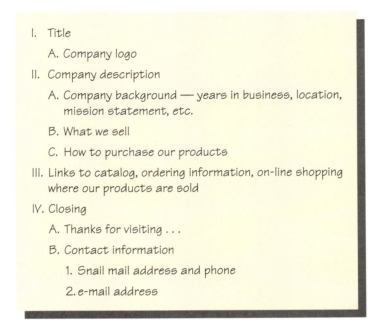

I. Title

   A. Company logo

II. Company description

   A. Company background — years in business, location, mission statement, etc.

   B. What we sell

   C. How to purchase our products

III. Links to catalog, ordering information, on-line shopping where our products are sold

IV. Closing

   A. Thanks for visiting . . .

   B. Contact information

      1. Snail mail address and phone

      2. e-mail address

FIGURE 5-2: The Nut Tree Company home page

Company logo

Header

Text

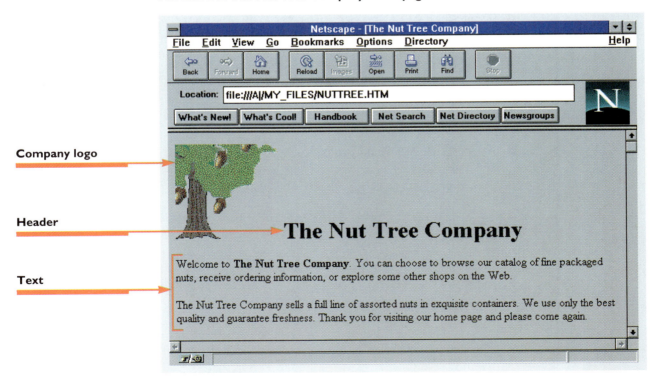

Structuring a Web page

For our purposes, we can divide HTML tags into two categories: structuring and formatting. **Structuring tags** mark and organize the elements of your page, such as the title, head, and body. See Table 5-1 for a description of structuring tags. **Formatting tags** provide control over how your page appears to Web users. ▶ Tags typically come in pairs and are bracketed by less than (<) and greater than (>) symbols (e.g., <HTML></HTML>). The first tag (e.g., <HTML>) in the pair "turns on" the structuring or formatting indicator while the second tag, the one with a forward slash, (e.g., </HTML>), "turns off" the indicator. These paired tags are **delimiters** that identify the beginning and end of a particular HTML structure or format. ▶ Use Notepad in Microsoft Windows to create your sample HTML page for The Nut Tree. To establish the organization of your Web page, start by entering the necessary structuring tags.

1 Double-click the **Accessories group icon** in Program Manager
The Accessories group window appears with a collection of program icons.

2 Double-click the **Notepad program icon** in the Accessories group window
The application window for Notepad appears, as shown in Figure 5-3. The blinking vertical line in the document window of Notepad, which is called an **insertion point** or **cursor**, indicates where text will appear when you type.

3 Type **<HTML>** and press **[Enter]**
The document window displays the text you typed, and the insertion point moves down one line.

4 Type **<HEAD>** and press **[Enter]**
The head tag appears on the second line of your page, and the insertion point moves down a line.

5 Type **<TITLE>The Nut Tree Company</TITLE>** and press **[Enter]**
This will appear in the Title bar of the Netscape application window when your Web page is displayed. At this point, the title and its tags appear on the third line, and the insertion point moves to the fourth line of your page.

6 Type **</HEAD>** and press **[Enter]**
The ending head tag appears on the fourth line, and the insertion point moves down a line. You are now ready to enter the tags for the body of the text.

7 Type **<BODY>,** press **[Enter]** twice, then type **</BODY>** and press **[Enter]**
The beginning and ending text body tags appear, separated by one blank line.

8 Type **<ADDRESS>**, press **[Enter]** twice, type **</ADDRESS>** and then press **[Enter]**, then type **</HTML>**
The beginning and ending address tags appear, separated by one blank line.

9 The closing structuring tag appears at the bottom of the page. Your screen should look similar to the one pictured in Figure 5-4

FIGURE 5-3:
The Notepad
application window

Insertion point
or cursor

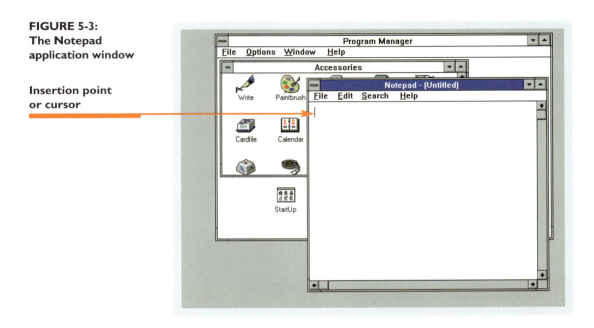

FIGURE 5-4:
Page with
structuring tags

Tags indicating
body of text

Tags indicating
address

Tag indicating type
of document

Tags indicating
page heading

Tag indicating
page title

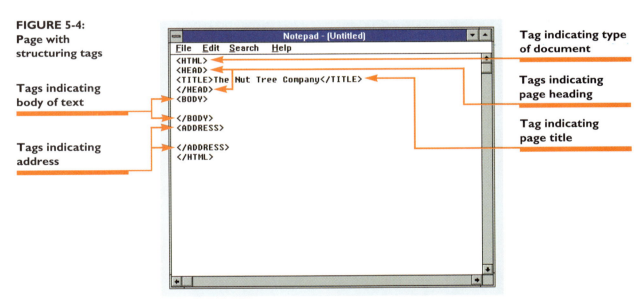

TABLE 5-1: Structuring tags

TAGS	IDENTIFIES DOCUMENT
<HTML></HTML>	Type
<HEAD></HEAD>	Heading
<TITLE></TITLE>	Title
<BODY></BODY>	Body
<ADDRESS></ADDRESS>	Address

QUICK

HTML ignores capital-
ization in tags. For
example, the tags
<TITLE></TITLE>
and <title></title>
would identify the title
of the Web page
equally well.■

Saving a file

To store an HTML page in Notepad permanently, you save it to a file on a disk. For information on saving an HTML page using Netscape, see the related topic "Saving a Web page with Netscape" later in this lesson. You should save your work every 10 to 15 minutes, especially before making significant changes to the page or before printing it. This way, you can return to the original file if you don't like the changes or something goes wrong with your computer during the printing process. You can save your file to the MY_FILES directory on your Student Disk. For more information about your Student Disk, refer to "Read This Before You Begin the World Wide Web." ▶ Name and save The Nut Tree home page to your Student Disk.

1   Click **File** on the menu bar, then click **Save**
The Save As dialog box appears, as shown in Figure 5-5. A brief description of each option in this dialog box is listed in Table 5-2.

2   Double-click the **File Name text box** and type **NUTTREE.HTM**
The name "NUTTREE. HTM" appears in the File Name text box.

3   Click the **Drives list arrow**, then click the drive that contains your Student Disk
Do not save the files on the internal hard disk, drive C, unless you are working on your own computer. If you created a MY_FILES directory in the Working with Windows section, you can save your files there. If you do not have a MY_FILES directory, skip Step 4 and continue with Step 5 to save the file to the a:\ directory on your Student Disk.

4   Double-click the **MY_FILES** directory in the Directories list box
The MY_FILES directory becomes the current directory.

5   Click **OK**
The Save As dialog box closes and the NUTTREE.HTM file is stored on your Student Disk.

FIGURE 5-5: Save As dialog box in Notepad

File Name text box

Directories list box

OK button

Cancel button

Drives list arrow

Save As

File Name:
*.txt

Directories:
a:\

a:\
home
my_files

OK

Cancel

Network...

Save File as Type:
Text Files [*.TXT]

Drives:
a:

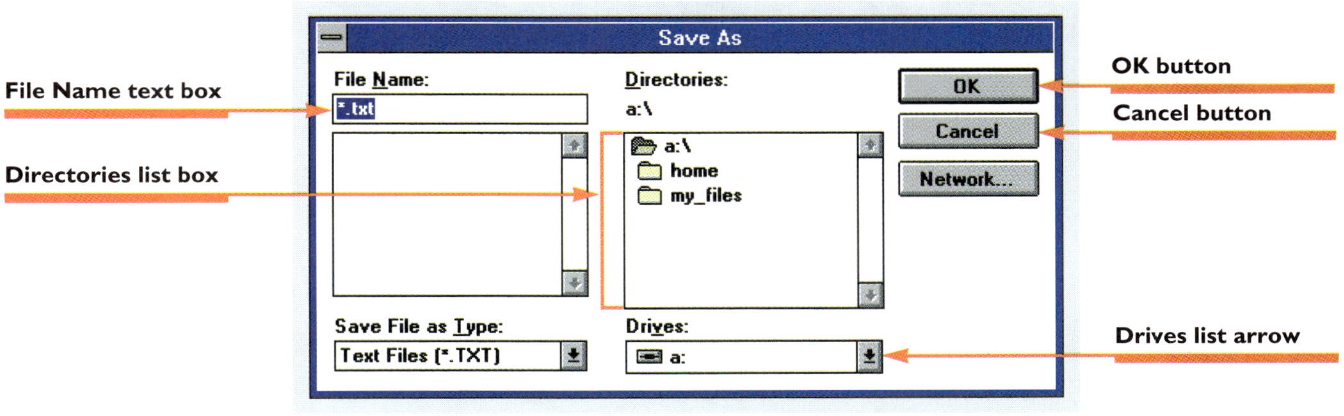

Saving a Web page with Netscape

Although you can't use Netscape to create or edit a Web page, it does offer the option to save Web pages that appear in your document window. Simply click File on the Netscape menu bar and then click Save as. The Save As dialog box opens and lets you select a drive and directory and enter a name for the file.

Netscape saves the page with all the HTML tags intact, as an HTML source file. **HTML source files** are simple text files that can be opened, viewed, and edited with any word processor. (To view the source file of the current page in Netscape but not edit it, simply click View on the Netscape menu bar, then click Source.)

Viewing the HTML structure of pages you find on the Web is a great way to discover innovative and useful page creation techniques. Editing the source file of a saved page can save you a lot of time and effort. For example, you might find a page containing a terrific collection of links to shopping malls on the Web. You can save the source file for this page using Netscape and then use a word processor (e.g., Notepad) to copy the list of links to your own Web page.

TABLE 5-2: Options in Save As dialog box in Notepad

OPTIONS	DESCRIPTION
File Name text box	Allows entry of file name
Directories list box	Allows selection of directory
Drives list box	Allows selection of drive
OK button	Saves the file and closes the Save As dialog box
Cancel button	Terminates the save operation and closes the Save As dialog box

Writing and formatting text

Now that you have identified the elements of the Web page, you need to write and format the text for each section. See the related topic "The do's and don't's of writing Web text" later in this lesson for some general rules to keep in mind while writing a home page. You will use the HTML formatting tags to control the way the text will appear when viewed with a Web browser. Table 5-3 describes some of the more popular formatting tags available in HTML. You can use these formatting tags to emphasize headings and key text, separate paragraphs and lines, specify a special type of treatment such as boldface, and insert ruler lines in a page. ▶ Type in the text for The Nut Tree home page, and use formatting tags to organize and emphasize the text.

1 Click the blank line between the structuring tags **<BODY>** and **</BODY>**
The insertion point appears at the beginning of this line.

2 Type **<H1>The Nut Tree Company</H1>** and press **[Enter]**
The <H1></H1> tags will cause the name of your company to appear as the largest heading in the page.

3 Type **<P>** and press **[Enter]**
The <P> tag creates a new paragraph. You are now ready to type the introductory paragraph of the page.

4 Type the following text, pressing **[Enter]** at the end of each line
Welcome to <B>The Nut Tree Company</B>. You can choose to browse our catalog of fine packaged nuts, receive ordering information, or explore some other shops on the Web.
The <B></B> tags cause the enclosed company title to display as bold-faced print when viewed with a Web browser.

5 Press **[Enter]** and type **<P>**, press **[Enter]** again, then type the following text, pressing **[Enter]** at the end of each line
The Nut Tree Company sells a full line of assorted nuts in exquisite containers. We use only the best quality ingredients and guarantee freshness. Thank you for visiting our home page and please come again.

6 Press **[Enter]** and type **<P>**
The text for the Web page has been inserted and tagged for formatting. Your page should look similar to the one pictured in Figure 5-6. Don't worry if your text does not wrap to the next line exactly like Figure 5-6.

7 Make sure your Student Disk is inserted in the appropriate drive, click **File** on the menu bar, then click **Save** to save the newly formatted Web page

FIGURE 5-6: Page with formatting tags and text

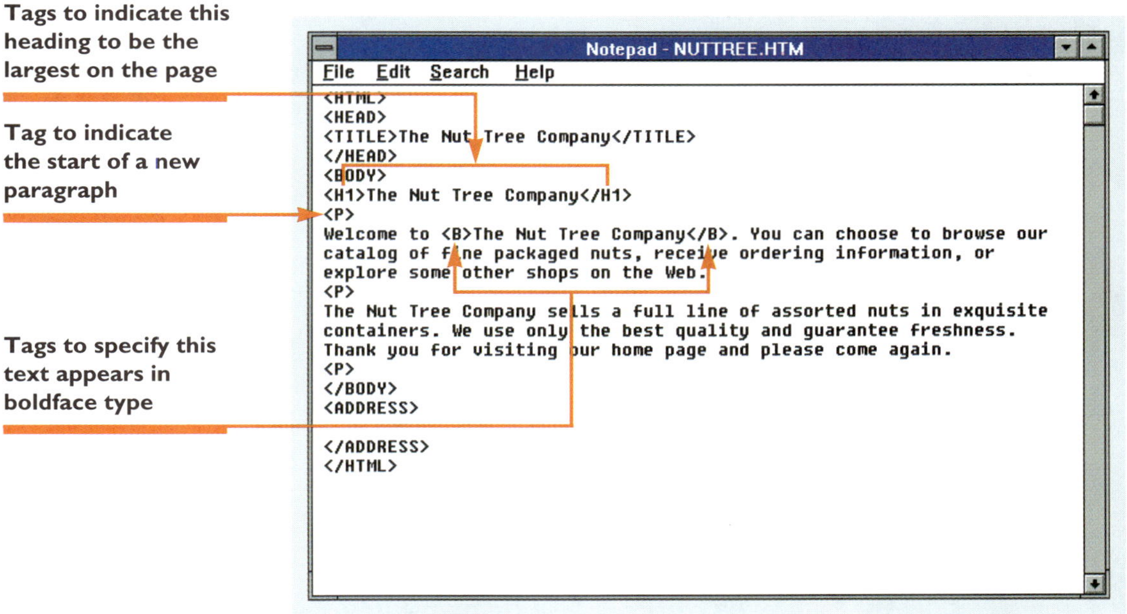

Tags to indicate this heading to be the largest on the page

Tag to indicate the start of a new paragraph

Tags to specify this text appears in boldface type

```
Notepad - NUTTREE.HTM
File  Edit  Search  Help

<HTML>
<HEAD>
<TITLE>The Nut Tree Company</TITLE>
</HEAD>
<BODY>
<H1>The Nut Tree Company</H1>
<P>
Welcome to <B>The Nut Tree Company</B>. You can choose to browse our
catalog of fine packaged nuts, receive ordering information, or
explore some other shops on the Web.
<P>
The Nut Tree Company sells a full line of assorted nuts in exquisite
containers. We use only the best quality and guarantee freshness.
Thank you for visiting our home page and please come again.
<P>
</BODY>
<ADDRESS>

</ADDRESS>
</HTML>
```

The do's and don't's of writing Web text

When writing the text for your home page, be sure to write clear, brief paragraphs of text. Web users are accustomed to reading short, concise text. Use emphasis sparingly; paragraphs with significant amounts of uppercase text, boldface, or italics can make the material hard to read. Be sure not to capitalize entire words or sentences as this is considered shouting on-line. Finally, before publishing your home page, check your spelling and grammar.

TABLE 5-3: HTML formatting tags

TAGS	DESCRIPTION
<H1></H1>	Largest heading size in the page — the next largest heading size is achieved by changing the number (e.g., <H2></H2> . . .<H6></H6>)
<P>	Starts a new paragraph by inserting a blank line
 	Starts a new line
<HR>	Inserts a ruler line
<B></B>	Boldface
<I></I>	Italics
<U></U>	Underline

Inserting links to other Web pages

The real power of a Web page lies in its ability to create links to other Web pages. You are already familiar with entering a URL address in your browser; the process of entering a URL in a Web page is very similar. ▶ Enter the links for two local pages prepared previously for the Nut Tree Company home page, then enter a link to a remote shopping site.

1 Make sure the insertion point appears just after the last <P> tag, press [Enter], then type <HR> and press [Enter] twice
The <HR> tag causes the Web page to display a ruler line when viewed with a Web browser. Pressing [Enter] twice causes a blank line to appear between the last tag and the current location of the insertion point.

2 Type <B>Selections:</B>, then press [Enter]
The word "Selections:" will now appear in boldface when viewed on a Web browser.

3 Type <P>, press [Enter], then type:
<A HREF=file:///a | /home/catalog.htm> The Nut Tree Catalog </A> features a collection of our best packaged nuts.
This entry called an <Anchor> links The Nut Tree home page to a local page, called CATALOG.HTM, on the A drive in the directory HOME on your Student Disk. See the related topic "Anchors" for more information.

4 Press [Enter] and type <P> and press [Enter] again. Now type:
<A HREF=file:///a | /home/orderinf.htm>Ordering information </A> for Nut Tree products - we'll ship anywhere in the U.S.
This anchor links The Nut Tree home page to a local page, called ORDERINF.HTM, on the A drive in the directory HOME on your Student Disk.

5 Press [Enter] and type <P> and press [Enter] again. Then type:
<A HREF="http://www.mecklerweb.com/imall/">The Internet Mall</A> is full of other places to shop on-line.
This Anchor provides a link from The Nut Tree home page to a remote Web site called The Internet Mall.

6 Press [Enter] and type <P>, press [Enter], type <P>, press [Enter], type <P>, and press [Enter] once more
These actions cause three blank lines to appear in your Web page when viewed with a Web browser.

7 If necessary, scroll down, then click the blank line between the <ADDRESS> tags and (being sure to press [Enter] at the end of each line) type:
The Nut Tree Company
501 East Main Street
Seattle, WA 99215
(800) BUY-NUTZ
NutTree@i-service.com
Your page should look similar to the one pictured in Figure 5-7. If not, edit it so that it matches.

8 Make sure your Student Disk is inserted in the appropriate drive and save the file to the MY_FILES directory on your Student Disk

FIGURE 5-7: Nut Tree home page with links to other pages and a contact address

Catalog link

Ordering
information link

Internet Mall link

Contact address

```
┌─────────────────────────────────────────────────────────────────┐
│ ▭         Notepad - NUTTREE.HTM                          ▽ ▲     │
├─────────────────────────────────────────────────────────────────┤
│ File   Edit   Search   Help                                       │
├─────────────────────────────────────────────────────────────────┤
│ The Nut Tree Company sells a full line of assorted nuts in exquisite │
│ containers. We use only the best quality and guarantee freshness. Thank you │
│ for visiting our home page and please come again.                 │
│ <P>                                                               │
│ <HR>                                                              │
│                                                                   │
│ <B>Selections:</B>                                               │
│ <P>                                                               │
│ <A HREF=file:///a|/home/catalog.htm>The Nut Tree Catalog</A> features a │
│ collection of our best packaged nuts.                            │
│ <P>                                                              │
│ <A HREF=file:///a|/home/orderinf.htm>Ordering information</A> for Nut Tree │
│ products - we'll ship anywhere in the US.                        │
│ <P>                                                              │
│ <A HREF="http://www.mecklerweb.com/imall/">The Internet Mall</A> is full of │
│ other places to shop on-line.                                    │
│ <P>                                                              │
│ <P>                                                              │
│ <P>                                                              │
│                                                                  │
│ </BODY>                                                          │
│ <ADDRESS>                                                        │
│ The Nut Tree Company<BR>                                         │
│ 501 East Main Street<BR>                                         │
│ Seattle, WA 99215<BR>                                            │
│ (800) BUY-NUTZ<BR>                                               │
│ NutTree@i-service.com                                            │
│ </ADDRESS>                                                       │
│ </HTML>                                                          │
└─────────────────────────────────────────────────────────────────┘
```

Anchors

The pair of <A></A> tags you typed in Step 5 indicates that this is a hypertext link or **<A>nchor**. The HREF= portion following the opening <A> tag links the URL "http://www.mecklerweb.com/imall/" to the text label The Internet Mall. The closing tag </A> specifies the end of the anchor. You are free to place any descriptive text you like after the hypertext link (e.g., "is full of other places to shop on-line").

Inserting graphics

A well-designed image or graphic can illustrate complicated information easily on a Web page. An image can also alert the viewer to important points of reference on a Web page. You insert an image on a Web page with an **image tag**. ▶ Melissa suggests that you place The Nut Tree's logo in front of the company's name on the home page. Use an image tag to insert a digitized version of The Nut Tree's logo into your home page.

STEPS ▶

1 If necessary, scroll up, then click immediately after the first <H1> tag in front of the header title
   The insertion point appears just in front of the title text, as shown in Figure 5-8.

2 Type **<IMG SRC="file:///a|/home/tree.gif" ALIGN=BOTTOM>**
   This image tag will cause The Nut Tree logo to be displayed on the same line as the firm's name when the home page is viewed with Netscape. The first letters in the tag, "IMG SRC," indicate that this is a screen image; the next section of the tag identifies the location and name of the image to be loaded; and the final attribute, "ALIGN=BOTTOM," specifies that the image is to be aligned with the bottom of the line of text next to which it appears.

3 Compare your modified header line with the one shown in Figure 5-9; if you mistyped any portion of it, correct the mistake using the edit keys

4 Make sure your Student Disk is inserted in the appropriate drive, and save the home page to the MY_FILES directory on your Student Disk
   The first draft of The Nut Tree home page is finished, and you are ready to view it and show it to Melissa, which you will do in the next lesson. First, exit Notepad.

5 Click **File** on the menu bar, then click **Exit**
   Notepad closes.

FIGURE 5-8: Correct location of the insertion point

Insertion point

FIGURE 5-9: The header line with an image tag

Modified header line

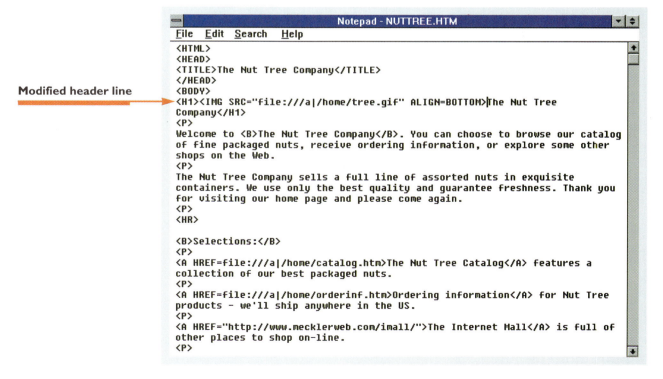

Viewing the page

Netscape provides an easy way to view pages stored on your local machine, on a network, or on a floppy disk. The File Open command on the File menu lets you quickly locate and load a local Web page for viewing. ▶ Melissa wants to see how the work is progressing on the sample home page for The Nut Tree. You'll use the File Open command in Netscape to show her.

STEPS ▶

1 Start Netscape

2 Click **File** on the menu bar, then click **File Open**
   The File Open dialog box appears, like the one shown in Figure 5-10. See Table 5-4 for a brief description of the options in this dialog box.

3 Click the **Drives list box arrow**
   A list of available disk drives appears. Find the drive that contains your Student Disk. In these instructions, we assume your Student Disk is in drive A.

4 Click **a:** to select drive A (or click **b:** if your Student Disk is in drive B)
   A list of the files on your Student Disk appears in the File Name list box.

5 Double-click the **MY_FILES** directory in the Directories list box
   The files stored in this directory appear in the File Name list box.

6 In the File Name list box, click **NUTTREE.HTM**, then click **OK**
   Netscape loads your Web page into the document window, as shown in Figure 5-11.

7 Examine the page to make sure it matches the figure, but don't click on any of the hypertext links yet

8 If your page is missing items shown in Figure 5-11, close Netscape, open Notepad, and open the file NUTTREE.HTM in the MY_FILES directory on your Student Disk, then make the necessary changes and save the file; launch Netscape and open the file again to check your changes

FIGURE 5-10: File Open dialog box

File Name text box

File Name list box

List Files of Type
list box

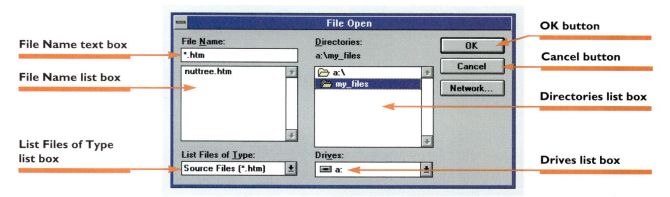

OK button

Cancel button

Directories list box

Drives list box

FIGURE 5-11:
Nut Tree page dis-
played in Netscape

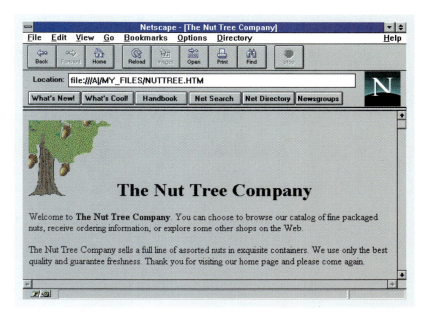

TABLE 5-4: The Open File dialog box options

OPTION	DESCRIPTION
File Name text box	Allows a file name to be entered
File Name list box	Enables a file name to be selected
Directories list box	Allows a different directory to be chosen
List Files of Type list box	Enables a file type to be selected
Drives list box	Allows a drive to be chosen
OK button	Opens the selected file
Cancel button	Cancels the operation and closes the dialog box

Testing the links

Just like other publications your company produces (e.g., brochures, flyers, newsletters, etc.), the quality of a Web page is important because it represents your company. So, along with excellent organization and high-quality writing, your page should contain accurate links. Because the Internet is constantly changing, you should test your links periodically to make sure they still work correctly. Once you have tested your home page, you can make arrangements to publish it. For information on how to publish a company page, see the related topic "Publishing a company home page" later in this lesson. ▶ You are now ready to test the links in The Nut Tree home page.

1   With The Nut Tree home page displayed in Netscape, click **The Nut Tree Catalog** link
    The document window changes to display the catalog page shown in Figure 5-12.

2   Click the **Back button** [Back] on the toolbar, and then click the **Ordering information** link
    A page with ordering information appears, as shown in Figure 5-13.

3   Click the **Back button** [Back] to return to The Nut Tree home page and then click **The Internet Mall** link
    The home page for The Internet Mall appears in your document window.

4   Click the **Home button** [Home] on the toolbar
    Your original home page appears in the document window.

5   Click **File** on the menu bar, then click **Exit**
    Netscape closes.

FIGURE 5-12:
The Nut Tree on-line
sample catalog

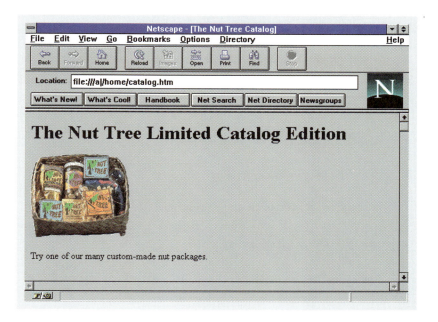

FIGURE 5-13: Ordering information for Nut Tree

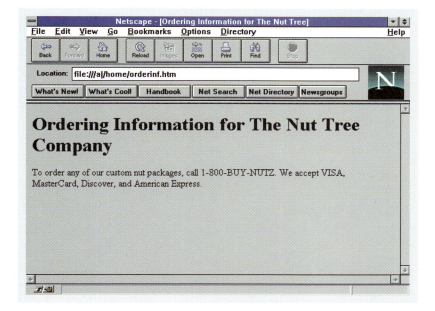

QUICK **TIP**

For further informa-
tion on creating your
own Web site, click
Help on the Netscape
menu bar, then click
How to Create Web
Services.■

TROUBLE?

If you receive an error
message when you
select a line on your
home page, open the
NUTTREE.HTM page
with Notepad and
check your link for
typing errors, make
any necessary correc-
tions, return to
Netscape, and select
the Reload button on
the toolbar to display
the corrected page.■

Publishing a company home page

There are three basic ways to publish a page on the Web: (1) rent or find free
space on a third-party Web server; (2) build your own server; or (3) hire someone
to build a server for you.

Renting space has the advantage of higher traffic and lower costs. Building your
own server gives you complete control over your presence on the Web but is quite
expensive. Hiring a contractor to build a Web site is even more expensive. However,
it is faster than learning how to create one yourself and provides complete control
over your presence in cyberspace.

TASKREFERENCE

TASK	METHOD
Tag page type	Type <HTML></HTML>
Tag page heading	Type <HEAD>*Heading Name*</HEAD>
Tag page title	Type <TITLE>*Page Title*</TITLE>
Tag page body	Type <BODY>*Body Text*</BODY>
Tag address	Type <ADDRESS>*Address*</ADDRESS>
Format top heading in page	Type <H1>*Heading*</H1>
Start a new paragraph	Type <P>
Start a new line	Type
Format a ruler line	Type <HR>
Format for bold-faced text	Type <B>*Text*</B>
Format for italic text	Type <I>*Text*</I>
Format for underlined text	Type <U>*Text*</U>
Insert links	Type <A HREF=*address*>*name of link*</A>
Insert graphic	Type <IMG SRC=*"graphic file name" Placement*>
View page	Click File, click Open File
Save page	Click File, click Save as
Save page within Netscape	Click File, click Save as
Test links	Click link
View HTML tags in page	Click View, click Source

CONCEPTS REVIEW

Label each of the HTML tags shown in Figure 5-14.

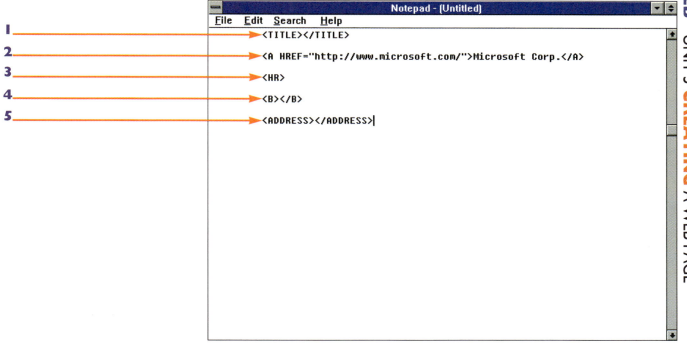

FIGURE 5-14

Match each of the terms below with the statement that best describes it function.

6 HTML

7 <P>

8 Web server

9 <H1></H1>

10 Tags

a. Computer system setup to provide access to Web pages

b. Special characters that structure and format Web pages

c. HyperText Markup Language

d. Inserts a blank line in a HTML page

e. Tags that indicate a top-level heading

Select the best answer from the list of choices.

11 The tag that identifies the beginning of an HTML page is

a. <P>

b. <HR>

c. <HEAD>

d. <HTML>

12 The tags that italicize text are

a. <ITALICS></ITALICS>

b. <WAVE></WAVE>

c. <I></I>

d. <B><I>

13 The first task in creating an HTML page is to write
   a. An outline
   b. A sample page
   c. An introductory paragraph
   d. A page title

14 All of the following are steps in planning an HTML page *except*
   a. Format text
   b. Test links
   c. Link to other pages
   d. Insert control markers

15 A home page should include all of the following *except*
   a. Large, clear images
   b. Introductory paragraph
   c. Links to other pages
   d. Contact address

16 You can use Netscape to view the HTML tags in a page by
   a. Selecting the View Tags command on the Edit menu
   b. Choosing the View Source command on the Edit menu
   c. Selecting the View HTML Code command on the Edit menu
   d. Choosing View on the menu bar, then Source

17 You can test the links in an HTML page by
   a. Clicking
   b. Double-clicking
   c. Dragging and dropping
   d. Closing

APPLICATIONSREVIEW

1 Structure a page.
   a. Open Notepad in the Accessories group window.
   b. Type in the following structuring tags as shown:

```
<HTML>
<HEAD>
<TITLE>My Home Page</TITLE>
</HEAD>
<BODY>

</BODY>
<ADDRESS>

</ADDRESS>
</HTML>
```

2 Save the file.
   a. Select File on the menu bar in Notepad, then choose the Save command.
   b. Type MYPAGE.HTM into the File Name text box.
   c. Specify the drive your Student Disk is in.
   d. Select the MY_FILES directory on your disk.
   e. Choose OK to save the file.

3 Write and format text.
   a. Insert the following between the beginning <BODY> and ending </BODY> tags:
      ```
      <H1>My Home Page</H1>
      <P>
      ```
   b. On the line below this text, type:
      Welcome to my home page. The following options will take you to my favorite spots for finding stuff on the Web. Enjoy!
      ```
      <P>
      ```
   c. Save the file to the MY_FILES directory on your Student Disk.

4 Insert links to other Web pages.
   a. Enter the following links and address to your home page:
      ```
      <HR>
      <B>Selections:</B>
      <P>
      <A HREF="http://www.w3.org/hypertext/DataSources/bySubject/Overview.htm">Using the Virtual Library</A>
      <P>
      <A HREF="http://www.netgen.com/cgi/comprehensive">Following the Wanderer</A>
      <P>
      <A HREF="http://webcrawler.cs.washington.edu/WebCrawler/WebQuery.html">Swinging with the WebCrawler</A>
      <P>
      <P>
      ```
   b. Insert the following between the ADDRESS tags:
      My Name
      My School or Company
      City, State Zip Code
      My Phone Number
      My E-mail Address
   c. Save the file to disk.

5 Insert graphics.
   a. Position the insertion point immediately after the first <H1> tag and type:
      ```
      <IMG SRC="file:///al/home/dog.gif" ALIGN=BOTTOM>
      ```
   b. Save the file to the MY_FILES directory on your Student Disk and exit Notepad.

6 View the page.

a. Start Netscape.

b. Load the MYPAGE.HTM file located in the MY_FILES directory on your Student Disk.

c. Examine the page to make sure it displays correctly. If you find that your page is displaying incorrectly, close Netscape, return to Notepad, open the page MYPAGE.HTM, and make the necessary corrections. Save the file and return to Netscape and open the file. If the page still fails to display correctly, repeat Step (c) until the problems are solved.

7 Test the links.

a. With My Home Page displayed in Netscape, click the Using the Virtual Library link. If you receive an error message, double-check your link in the MYPAGE.HTM file, make any changes necessary using Notepad, and return to Netscape and the page to test the link again. Repeat this process until the link works correctly.

b. Perform the same process outlined in Step (a) on the two untested links in your page.

c. Click the Home button ![Home] on the toolbar.

Your original home page appears in the document window.

INDEPENDENT
CHALLENGE 1

Do the following to create a home page for a friend:

1 Open Notepad and insert the structuring tags for the elements listed below. (These elements were derived from an outline given to you by your friend.)

```
<HTML>
<HEAD>
<TITLE>Linda's Home Page</TITLE>
</HEAD>
<BODY>

</BODY>
<ADDRESS>

</ADDRESS>
</HTML>
```

2 Save the file on your Student Disk in the MY_FILES directory with the file name "Linda.htm."

3 Enter and format the text shown below between the BODY tags in your page.

```
<H1>My Home Page</H1>
<P>
```
Hello! I am Linda and this is my home page. It contains some of my favorite spots on the Web. Please e-mail me at the address below if you know about other cool places to visit.
```
<P>
```

4 Insert these hypertext links directly below the text you entered:
```
<P>
<A HREF="http://www.mecklerweb.com/" >Meckler
```
Web</A> is a great place to find information about the Internet and the Web.
```
<P>
<A HREF="http://lcweb.loc.gov/homepage/lchp.html">
```
The Library of Congress</A> has cool exhibits and government-related information.
```
<P>
```

5 Insert the contact information shown below in between the ADDRESS tags, then save the file as Linda.HTM.
Linda_T@bullwinkle.edu

6 Use Netscape to view the page. It should look like the page shown in Figure 5-15. If not, use Notepad to make the necessary corrections.

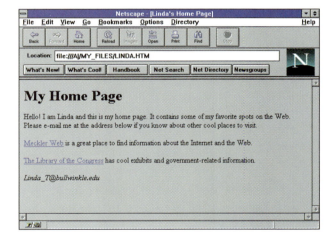

FIGURE 5-15: Linda's home page

7 Test the hypertext links by clicking one and then returning to the page to select the other one. If problems arise, use Notepad to check your hypertext entries for mistyping.

8 Print a copy of the page using Netscape.

INDEPENDENT
CHALLENGE 2

Melissa Jones is considered a movie aficionado amongst her friends and family. Complete the following steps to create a Web page that features Melissa's favorite movie resources on the Web for her friends and family to access:

1 Create an outline for the Web page, including a page title, an introductory paragraph, a list of links, and a contact address.

2 Insert structuring tags for each element based on your outline.

3 Save the file to your Student Disk in the MY_FILES directory.

4 Write and format several paragraphs describing why Melissa likes these movie resources. Be sure to use boldface at least once.

5 Insert the following hypertext links to remote Web sites:
```
<P>
<A HREF="http://www.cm.cf.ac.uk/Movies/">Cardiff
Movie Database browser</A> allows searching for movie
titles, actors, directors, etc.
<P>
<A HREF="http://www.disney.com/">Buena Vista
Movie Plex</A>, a home page for the movie studio.
<P>
<A HREF="http://www.mca.com/">Universal
Pictures</A>
<P>
```

6 Use Netscape to view the page. It should look similar to the one shown in Figure 5-16. If not, use Notepad to correct any typing mistakes and view it again.

7 Verify that the hypertext links are working correctly.

8 From Netscape, print a copy of the page.

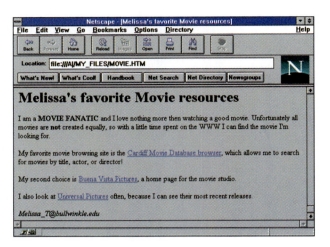

FIGURE 5-16: Melissa's Web page of favorite movie resources

INDEPENDENT
CHALLENGE 3

You are almost all packed and ready to leave for your Peace Corps teaching position in South Africa. You realize you will be very busy once you begin your new career, and you doubt you will have time to write long letters to friends and family. You decide to create a Web page that friends and family can access to keep abreast of how you are faring in your new life. Design and create a Web page that will provide them with news on what you are learning, where you live, what you have been eating, and requests for care packages. When you finish, print a copy of the page from Netscape.

INDEPENDENT
CHALLENGE 4

Create a Web page with links to business resources on the Web that you think John Prescott, president of the Words and Wisdom PR firm, will find useful. Use one of the search methods from Unit 4 to locate a Web page with a list of business resources, save it with Netscape, and use a word processor to edit and copy five of the links for use in your own custom page. Print a copy of the page from Netscape when you finish.

Exploring OTHER INTERNET RESOURCES

The World Wide Web is the fastest growing segment of the Internet. Nonetheless, the Internet offers other utilities and informational resources beyond the World Wide Web, such as electronic mail, Usenet news, Gopher, and FTP (File Transfer Protocol). Electronic mail, or e-mail, and newsgroups allow you to communicate with other Internet users interactively. Gopher servers enable you to explore information on the Internet through a sophisticated system of menus. Finally, FTP allows you to transfer files on the Internet to your own computer for your personal use. ▶ Since hypertext links can point to other Internet services, you may have already ventured beyond the edge of the Web. This appendix provides a brief overview of the most common resources you are likely to encounter outside the Web. It also explains how to use Netscape Navigator 1.1 to access these information sources. ▶

E-mail

Electronic mail, or **e-mail**, is a system used to send and receive messages electronically. E-mail is by far the most popular service on the Internet. Internet users send and receive hundreds of thousands of messages daily using e-mail. At present, Netscape supports only the sending but not the receiving of e-mail. ▶ Before you can send an e-mail message with Netscape, you must obtain an e-mail address and the name of your mail server. Once you have this information, select Options on the Netscape menu bar, then click the Preferences command. The Preferences dialog box appears. Select the Mail and News option from the Set Preferences On list box to display the form shown in Figure A-1. Fill in the Mail (SMTP) Server, Your Name, Your E-mail, and Your Organization text boxes with the correct information.

FIGURE A-1: Mail and News option in the Preferences dialog box

Set Preferences On drop-down list

Fill in appropriate information before sending e-mail

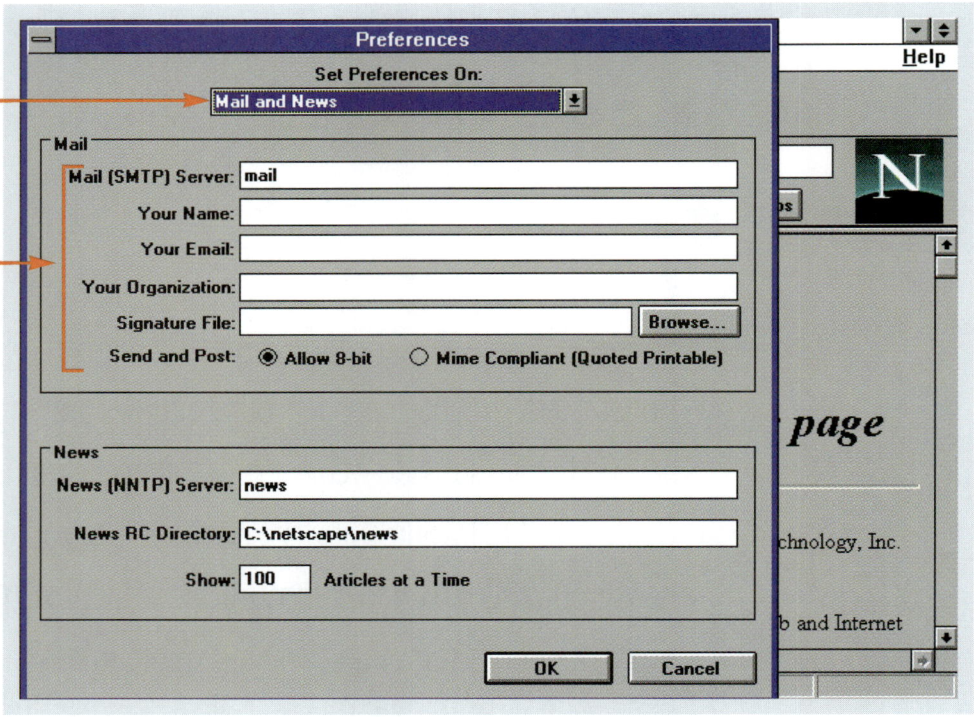

To send e-mail, either select File on the menu bar and then Mail Document, or press [Ctrl][M]. If the information was entered correctly in Preferences, a Send Mail/Post News dialog box appears, as shown in Figure A-2. This dialog box lets you enter and send an e-mail message. Table A-1 describes the options in this dialog box.

FIGURE A-2: Send Mail/Post News dialog box

e-mail address of
recipient goes here

Briefly describes
message contents

Type body of message
here

Click to cancel sending
the message

Click to mail message

Click to include contents
of current Web page

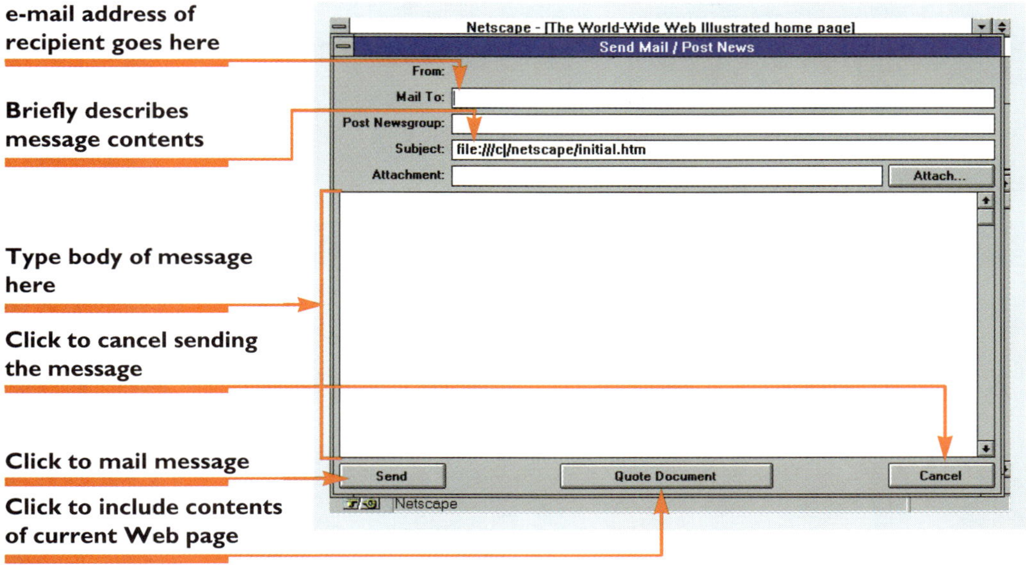

QUICK TIP

If you are using
Netscape on a com-
puter other than your
own, be sure to
remove your e-mail
address from the
Preferences dialog
box before exiting
Netscape. Otherwise,
the next user may
inadvertently use
your e-mail address
to send messages. ■

TABLE A-1: Send Mail/Post News dialog box options

OPTION	DESCRIPTION
Mail To text box	Specifies the e-mail address of the person you want to send a message to
Post Newsgroup text box	Posts the message to a designated newsgroup (for more information on newsgroups, see the Usenet newsgroups sections later in this appendix)
Subject text box	Allows a brief description of the content of your message
Attachment text box	Allows a description of a separate file that you want sent along with the e-mail message
Attach . . . button	Specifies which file to send along with the e-mail message
Message text box	Allows entry of the message
Send button	Transmits the message to the recipient
Quote Document button	Includes the contents of the current Web page into your message
Cancel button	Terminates the message and closes the Send Mail/Post News dialog box

Frequently used e-mail addresses can be added to your URL Bookmark list. Once
they are entered as bookmarks, you can simply open the Bookmark list and select
an e-mail address to open the Send Mail/Post News dialog box; Netscape then
automatically enters the address of the recipient in the Mail To text box. This will
help you organize and access these addresses more easily.

Subscribing to Usenet newsgroups

Usenet is a system of over 7,000 **newsgroups** where Internet users can meet to discuss particular topics. There are thousands of newsgroups on almost every conceivable subject. See Table A-2 for a list of typical Usenet news categories of topics.

TABLE A-2: Common Usenet Newsgroup Categories

CATEGORY	DESCRIPTION	EXAMPLES
alt	Alternative newsgroups of many different types	alt.activism, alt.conspiracy.jfk, alt.wolves
comp	Computer science and related topics	comp.graphics, comp.ai, comp.protocols.tcp-ip
misc	Topics that don't fit any of the other categories, or that bridge two or more categories	misc.jobs.offered, misc.forsale, misc.education
news	Discussions of Usenet itself	news.announce.newusers, news.answers, news.future
rec	Discussion about recreational activities	rec.humor.funny, rec.humor, rec.arts.sf.announce
sci	Scientific discussions	sci.chem.organomet, sci.geo.geology, sci.math.symbolic
soc	Social and political issues	soc.culture.indian, soc.college.grad, soc.religion.bahai
talk	Controversial topics	talk.bizarre, talk.environment, talk.politics.theory

You can participate in a newsgroup discussion by either sending a message in response to an article you are reading, or by submitting an article of your own. This activity is called **posting**. For example, a newsgroup dedicated to Elvis Presley may feature an article on the author's preference for the older Elvis over the younger Elvis. The article might then be followed by a number of responses from other Elvis aficionados indicating their agreement or disagreement with the author's article. ▶ Netscape includes a very full-featured newsreader that makes it easy to follow and participate in the Usenet discussions. However, before you can use this newsreader, Netscape must be assigned a news server. A **news server** is a computer that stores the Usenet newsgroup articles. It enables you to retrieve and post messages to the newsgroup. ▶ If you attempt to launch the newsreader without a news server, you will receive an error message. The News portion of the Preferences dialog box lets you assign a news server to Netscape. Check with your instructor or lab support person to determine if a news server is available and if your installation of Netscape has been set up to use it.

To start the news reader in Netscape, click the Newsgroups button [Newsgroups] on the directory button bar or select Directory on the menu bar and then select Go to Newsgroups. The opening page in the document contains a list of the newsgroups that you are currently following or **subscribed** to, like the one shown in Figure A-3. You can use the options on this page to subscribe to additional newsgroups or unsubscribe from newsgroups that no longer interest you.

FIGURE A-3: Opening page of Netscape's newsreader

Newsgroups Netscape automatically subscribes you to

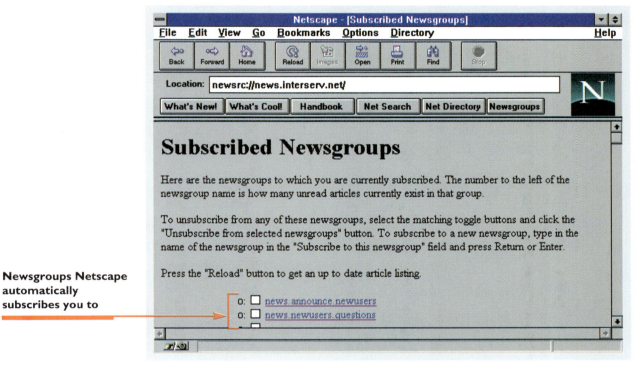

By default, Netscape automatically **subscribes** you to three newsgroups, "news.announce.newusers," "news.newusers.questions," and "news.answers." The number to the left of each newsgroup name indicates how many articles in the newsgroup you haven't read yet. If you want to subscribe to another newsgroup (i.e., add a newsgroup to the list on the opening newsgroup page), type the name of the newsgroup in the Subscribe to this newsgroup text box and press [Enter]. To unsubscribe from a newsgroup (i.e., remove it from your opening newsgroup page), select the check box in front of the newsgroup name you want to remove and click the Unsubscribe from selected newsgroups button on the lower portion of the page. ▶ If you don't know the name of the newsgroup(s) you want to subscribe to, you can search the available groups by clicking the View all newsgroups button at the bottom of the page. A search form appears that lets you enter key words to identify newsgroup(s) that interest you, like the one shown in Figure A-4. Simply type the key word(s) in the text box that is (are) likely to appear in the title of the newsgroup you are looking for (e.g., music), and then press [Enter]. Netscape displays a list of newsgroups whose titles contain your key word(s).

FIGURE A-4: Newsgroups list search form

Search newsgroups text box

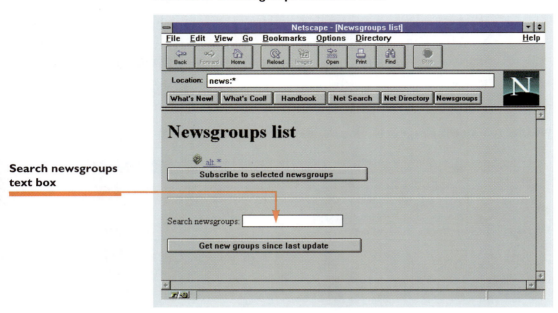

Reading and posting newsgroup articles

To see a listing of the topics in a newsgroup, simply click the newsgroup's name in the opening page of the Netscape newsreader. A newsgroup page appears with an outline of articles and responses, like the one shown in Figure A-5.

FIGURE A-5: Sample newsgroup page

Show Read Articles button

Catchup All Articles button

Subscribe button

Subscribed Newsgroups button

Article title

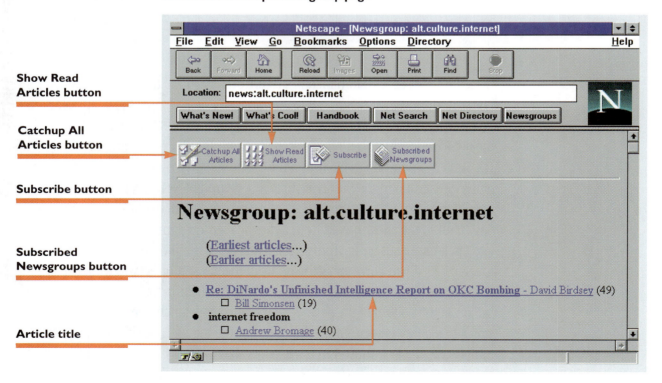

This hierarchically arranged outline indents the name of respondents below article titles to indicate the **thread** or flow of the conversation. This organizational scheme provides an easy way to follow the discussion stimulated by the article. You can quickly scan the outline to see the extent of discussion that has taken place on each article. It's a good idea to follow a newsgroup for a while before posting a message. This ensures that you understand the context of the discussion before contributing to it. ▶ Netscape's newsreader provides a row of list buttons at the top and bottom of every page that list articles. The **list buttons** let you perform a number of tasks. For a description of these buttons and the tasks they let you perform, see Table A-3.

TABLE A-3: Descriptions of List buttons

BUTTON NAME	BUTTON ICON	DESCRIPTION
Catchup All Articles	Catchup All Articles	Marks all articles as if you read them
Show Read Articles	Show Read Articles	Displays only the articles you haven't viewed yet
Subscribe	Subscribe	Subscribes you to the newsgroup, adding the name and location of the newsgroup to a list maintained by Netscape Navigator
Subscribed Newsgroups	Subscribed Newsgroups	Displays a list of the newsgroups you are currently subscribed to

To view an article or response, simply click it. The article appears in your document window, similar to the one shown in Figure A-6. Like the page that lists newsgroups, newsgroup article pages provide a set of buttons that let you navigate among the newsgroup's articles and respond to an article. Table A-4 describes the function of these **article buttons**.

FIGURE A-6: Sample article page

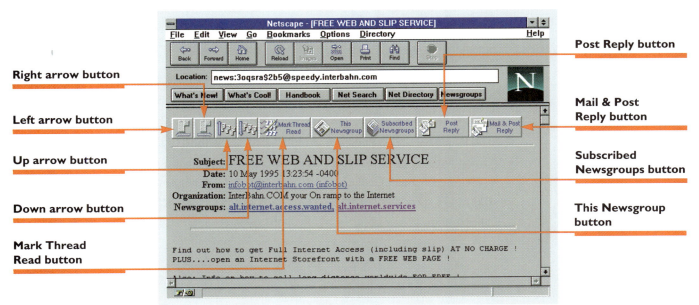

TABLE A-4: Article button descriptions

BUTTON NAME	BUTTON ICON	DESCRIPTION
Left arrow		Displays the previous article in the thread
Right arrow		Displays the next article in the thread
Up arrow		Displays the first article in the thread of the last topic
Down arrow		Displays the first article in the thread of the next topic
Mark Thread Read		Marks the thread as having been read
This Newsgroup		Displays the newsgroup list page
Subscribed Newsgroups		Opens the subscribe/unsubscribe page with a list of your current newsgroup subscriptions
Post Reply		Opens the Send Mail/Post News dialog box and lets you enter and send your message as a response to the current posting appearing in the document window
Mail & Post Reply		Opens the Send Mail/Post News dialog box so you can send a message simultaneously to the newsgroup and send a private e-mail message to the article's author

You can use Netscape to post a message or article in a newsgroup if you have an e-mail address and have entered it in the Preferences dialog box. To post a newsgroup message, click the Post Reply button that appears at the top of your document window. The Send Mail/Post News dialog box opens. Simply type a short subject in the Subject text box, type your message or article in the Message text box, and click the Send button just below the Message text box to submit your article to the newsgroup.

Gopher

Another way to access information on the Web and the Internet is to use a service called **Gopher**, which organizes different on-line resources into easy-to-use menus. To use Gopher, you need to access a **Gopher server**, several of which are available on various Internet hosts. ▶ Once you gain access to a Gopher server, you can select a menu item from the top layer or main menu. In Netscape, Gopher menu items appear as links, as shown in Figure A-7. You select a menu item the same way you select a Web link, by clicking it. This action typically causes a submenu to appear. Since there can be many layers of menus between you and the information you want, this selection process has come to be known as **tunneling**.

FIGURE A-7: Sample Gopher menu

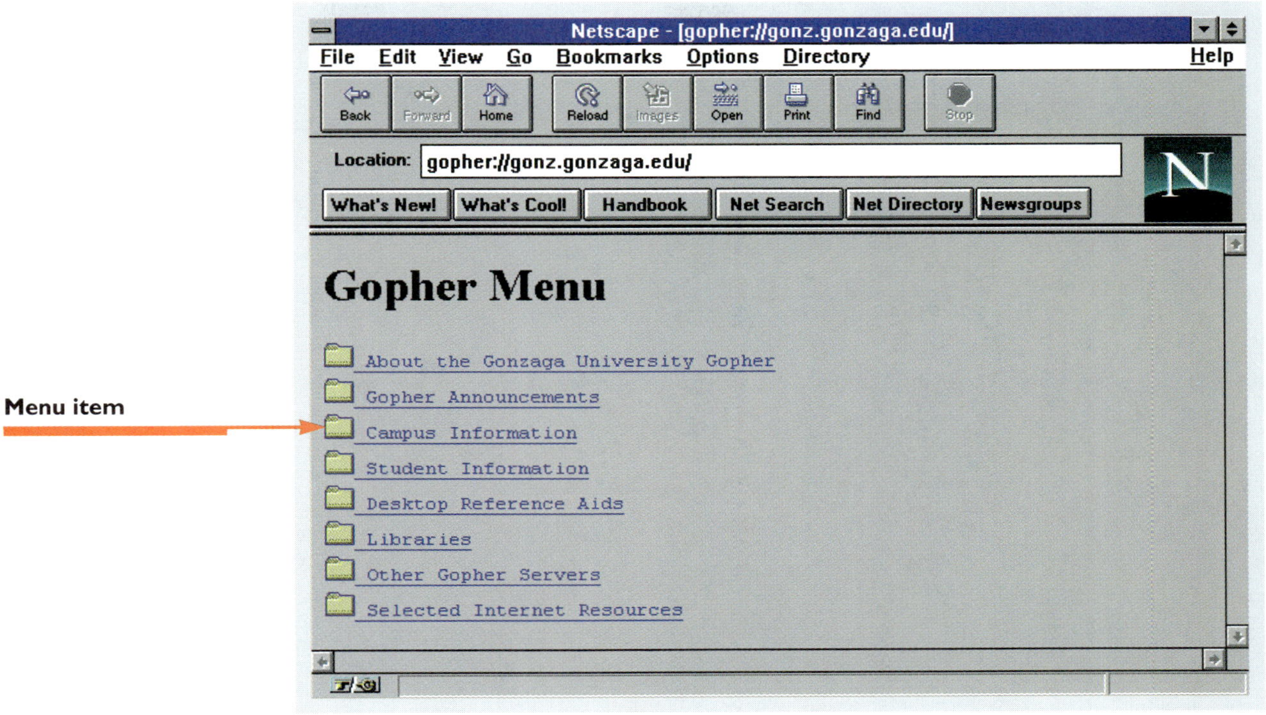

Menu item

All Gopher servers are connected via their menu items. So, when you choose an item on a Gopher menu, you might end up seeing the next menu on a Gopher server halfway around the world. This network of Gopher servers is often called **Gopherspace**. ▶ Gopherspace can be fun to tunnel through (explore), but when you want to locate information quickly, you should use a Gopher search engine. **Gopher search engines** automatically scan all the menu items in Gopherspace for the key word(s) you enter. Many Gopher sites on the Internet offer search engines with search forms, like the one shown in Figure A-8.

FIGURE A-8: Gopher search form

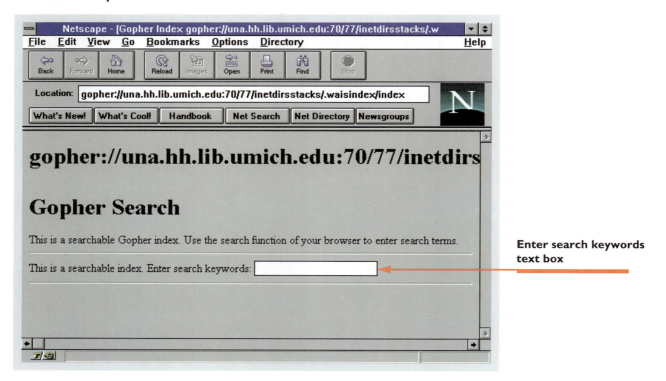

Enter search keywords text box

FTP

File Transfer Protocol (FTP) is a communication standard that lets you retrieve and send files over the Internet. You can use Netscape to FTP files to anywhere in the world. To transmit a file, simply click the Open button, type FTP:// followed by the name of the site and file you desire. See Figure A-9 for an example. You will also encounter hypertext links to FTP sites in Web pages. To verify that a particular hypertext link is an FTP link, point at it with your mouse and check the progress bar to see if the URL begins with FTP://. To use an FTP link, simply click it.

FIGURE A-9: Using Netscape to access an FTP site

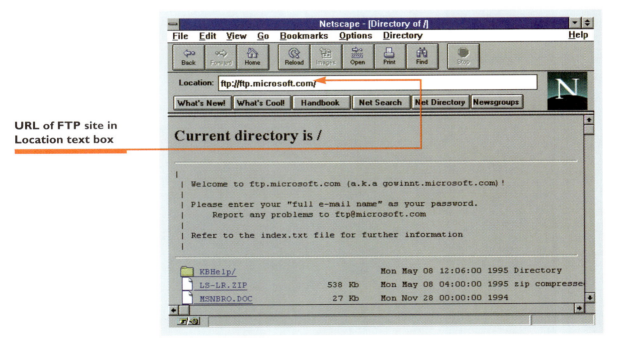

URL of FTP site in Location text box

The collection of FTP sites on the Internet is gigantic. When you want to find a particular file, it can be like trying to find a grain of sand in a desert. **ArchiePlex** is a program that scans all the known FTP sites on the Internet and compiles a list of files you can retrieve. It is a Web-based version of a similar Internet program called **Archie**. ▶ Unlike Archie (which requires another Internet client called Telnet — see the related topic "Telnet," which follows), ArchiePlex is designed to work with a Web browser like Netscape. It provides an ArchiePlexForm to fill out. The entries you make in the form are used to find the location of files related to your search topic. You can use the searching techniques described in Unit 3 to locate a list of ArchiePlex sites on the Web.

Telnet

Telnet is an Internet utility that lets you connect to and use a remote computer. Netscape requires a **Telnet client program**, an application that allows Netscape to use Telnet to connect to and communicate with a remote computer. There are a number of public domain and commercial Telnet client programs available.

You can use the ArchiePlex service described above to locate and FTP a Telnet client program for use with Netscape. Check with your instructor or lab support person for additional details before attempting to add a Telnet client program to Netscape.

As with e-mail addresses, you can save the addresses of your favorite FTP sites to the Bookmark list in Netscape. You can add them to the Bookmark list the same way you add standard Web addresses. You may want to organize them under a category called FTP in your Bookmark list for quick identification, as shown in Figure A-10.

FIGURE A-10: Bookmark list showing FTP category

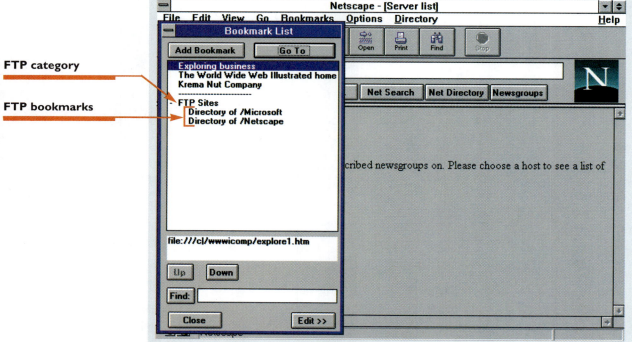

FTP category

FTP bookmarks

Glossary

Active application   The application or program that is running. See also *Task List*.

Active window   A window that you are currently using. If a window is active, its title bar changes color to differentiate it from other windows.

Address   Unique string of text that identifies the location of a Web page on the World Wide Web. Also known as the Uniform Resource Locator (URL).

Application   A task-oriented software program that you use for a particular kind of work, such as word processing or database management. Microsoft Access, Microsoft Excel, and Microsoft Word are all applications.

ArchiePlex   A program that scans for and compiles a list of files you can retrieve using FTP. It is the Web-based version of a similar Internet program called Archie. *See also* File Transfer Protocol.

Arpanet   A program sponsored by the US Department of Defense in 1969 that created and maintained a network of four computers built and designed to withstand nuclear attack. As non-military and educational institutions began using Arpanet, the network rapidly developed into what today is known as the Internet.

Article   A message posted to a newsgroup by an Internet user that furthers the discussion on the newsgroup's topic. *See also* Newsgroup and Post.

Article buttons   The Netscape newsreader buttons that enable you to navigate among the newsgroups articles in a thread and respond to an article. *See also* Article, Newsreader, and Thread.

Bookmark   A feature of Netscape Navigator which enables you to mark Web pages of particular interest to you for future reference and easy access.

Bookmark list   A collection of bookmarks which can be organized into easy to use categories.

Click   To press and release the mouse button quickly in one motion.

Command button   In a dialog box, a button that carries out an action. A command button usually has a label that describes its action, such as Cancel or Help. If the label is followed by an ellipsis, clicking the button displays a dialog box.

Command prompt   Symbol used to represent the drive and directory at which you can launch a program (usually C:\> is called the DOS command prompt).

Content-oriented search   A search method which is most effective when searching for information on a specific topic. Requires a search engine. *See also* Search engine.

Cursor   The blinking vertical line in the Notepad document window which indicates where text will appear when you type. Also referred to as the insertion point.

Cybershop   A place on the World Wide Web where a company markets its products and services. Also referred to as an on-line storefront.

Delimiters   Specially paired tags that identify the beginning and end of a particular HTML structure or format. *See also* Structuring tags, Formatting tags, and HyperText Markup Language (HTML).

Desktop   An electronic version of a desk that provides workspace for different computing tasks on a computing screen.

Dialog box   A window that appears temporarily to request information. Many dialog boxes have options you must choose before Windows can carry out a command.

Directory   Part of a structure for organizing your files on a disk. A directory can contain files and other directories (called subdirectories).

Directory button bar   Contains buttons that provide links connecting you to useful sites on the World Wide Web and the Internet.

Document window   Displays the current Web page. *See also* Web page and Web document.

Domain name   The second part of a URL which indicates the name and type of institution that owns the Web site that is being accessed. *See also* Uniform Resource Locator (URL) and Web site.

Double-click   To press and release the mouse button twice quickly.

Drag   To point at an item, press and hold the left mouse button, move the mouse to a new location, then release the mouse button.

E-zine   An electronic magazine characterized by stunning imagery and brief articles.

Electronic mail (e-mail)   A system used to send and receive messages electronically.

Electronic publishers   Organizations that provide books, magazines, and newspapers on-line.

FedWorld   A subject-oriented catalog with links to hundreds of Federal sites. *See also* Subject-oriented catalog.

File Transfer Protocol (FTP)   A communication standard that allows you to retrieve and send files over the Internet.

Followed link   A textual link that appears in purple, indicating you have already selected that link and viewed the corresponding Web page. *See also* HyperText links.

Formatting tag   A type of HTML tag that provides control over how your Web page appears to users. For example, formatting tags can be used to specify a special type treatment, such as boldface or italics. *See also* HyperText Markup Language (HTML).

Frequently Asked Questions (FAQ)   An on-line Help feature found in Netscape's Help menu that Netscape Communications Corporation updates on a regular basis. It lists the answers to commonly asked questions from Netscape users.

Gopher   An Internet tool which organizes different on-line resources into easy to use menus.

Gopher search engine   A software program that automatically scans all the menu items in Gopherspace for keyword(s) you enter into a search form. *See also* Gopherspace.

Gopher server   A computer that runs a software program that enables Internet users to access and use Gopher. *See also* Gopher.

Gopherspace   The network of Gopher servers available on the Internet. *See also* Gopher server.

Graphical user interface (GUI)   A software program that works hand in hand with the MS-DOS operating system to control the basic operation of a computer and the programs that run on it.

Group   A collection of applications and accessories within Program Manager.

Guide   A navigational aid that lists and describes new, unusual, and outstanding Web pages. Also referred to as tour guides or travel guides. Examples of guides would be Spry City, Global Network Navigator, and Edge of the Web. *See also* Guide-oriented search.

Guide-oriented search   A search method used when trying to locate something new or unusual on the Web. *See also* Guide.

Home page   The initial Web page Netscape loads each time you launch the program. *See also* Web page.

Horizontal scroll bar   Allows you to quickly move left and right through a Web page.

HTML source files   Simple text files that include the HTML tags and can be opened, viewed, and edited with any word processor. *See also* HyperText Markup Language (HTML).

http   The first four letters found in each URL, and stands for HyperText Transport Protocol. *See also* Uniform Resource Locator (URL) and HyperText Transport Protocol (HTTP).

Hyperlinks   Enable you to open related Web pages by clicking them with your mouse. You can use these links to follow a topic from page to page across the Web without regard to where the pages reside. Hyperlinks that appear as text are highlighted in a special color (usually blue) and underlined. Hyperlinks may also appear as graphics. Also referred to as hypertext links or links.

Hyperregions   Graphical links in a Web page that when clicked, connect you to a group of related Web pages.

Hypertext links   Enable you to open related Web pages by clicking them with your mouse. You can use these links to follow a topic from page to page across the Web without regard to where the pages reside. Hypertext links that appear as text are highlighted in a special color (usually blue) and underlined. Hypertext links may also appear as graphics. Also referred to as hyperlinks or links.

HyperText Markup Language (HTML)   The programming language used to describe the general structure of a Web page. HTML uses special characters, called tags, to enable your browser to properly display the contents of a Web page. *See also* Structuring tags and Formatting tags.

HyperText Transport Protocol (HTTP)   The communication standard established for the World Wide Web that ensures every computer accessing the World Wide Web is talking the same language when sending and receiving Web pages.

Icon   A picture symbol used to represent a command.

Image tag   An HTML tag used to insert a graphical image in a Web page. *See also* HyperText Markup Language (HTML).

Insertion point   The blinking vertical line in the Notepad document window which indicates where text will appear when you type. Also referred to as the cursor.

Internet A collection of networks that connect computers all over the world together using phone lines, coaxial cables, fiber optic cables, satellites, and other telecommunications media. *See also* Network.

Keyword(s) Words entered into a search form that represent a topic in which you are interested in. *See also* Search form.

Launch To start a program or application so you can use it.

Links Enable you to open related Web pages by clicking them with your mouse. You can use these links to follow a topic from page to page across the Web without regard to where the pages reside. Links that appear as text are highlighted in a special color (usually blue) and underlined. Links may also appear as graphics. Also referred to as hyperlinks or hypertext links.

List buttons The buttons provided by Netscape's newsreader that allow you to post an article, subscribe, and unsubscribe to a newsgroup. *See also* Newsreader.

Load a Web page Refers to the process of finding and opening a Web page once its link has been selected. *See also* Hypertext link.

Location text box Displays the URL of the current Web page appearing in the document window. *See also* Uniform Resource Locator (URL).

Location-oriented search A search method often conducted using maps. This method is best used when attempting to locate Web sites in a specific geographical area. *See also* Web site and Map.

Map A search tool which displays locations of Web sites geographically. This type of search tool works well when searching for Web sites in a particular geographical region. Many of the graphical links on maps are hyperregions. Examples of maps would be the Virtual Tourist and the Wanderer, a directory service of sites organized by geographical location. *See also* Web site, Location-oriented search, Links, and Hyperregion.

Marc Andreessen A former student of the University of Illinois in Urbana-Champaign who created the first graphical Web browser, Mosaic, and who now co-owns Netscape Communications Corporation, the developers of Netscape Navigator. *See also* Mosaic and Web browser.

Maximize To enlarge a window so it takes up the entire screen. There is usually a Maximize button in the upper-right corner of a window.

Menu A list of available commands in an application window.

Menu bar Displays the names of the menus that contain Netscape commands. Clicking a menu name on the menu bar displays a list of commands from which you can choose.

Minimize To reduce the size of a window. There is usually a Minimize button in the upper-right corner of a window. Double-clicking the Minimize button shrinks the window to an icon.

Mosaic The first graphical Web browser developed by Marc Andreessen while he was a student at the University of Illinois in Urbana-Champaign. *See also* Web Browser.

Mouse A hand-held input device that you roll on your desk to position the mouse pointer on the Windows desktop. *See also* Mouse pointer.

Mouse pointer The arrow-shaped cursor on the screen that follows the movement of the mouse as you roll the mouse on your desk. You use the mouse pointer to select items, choose commands, start applications, and word process in applications. The shape of the mouse pointer changes depending on the application and the task being executed.

Netscape Navigator 1.1 for Windows The newest and most popular Web browser developed by Netscape Communications Corporation. *See also* Web browser.

Network Two or more computers connected together in order to exchange and share data.

Newsgroup A collection of Internet users meeting electronically to discuss a particular topic of interest.

Newsreader A program that enables you to post and retrieve Usenet newsgroup articles. *See also* Usenet.

News server A computer that stores the Usenet newsgroup articles. *See also* Usenet.

Notepad A simple text editor that lets you create memos, record notes, or edit text files. It is a Microsoft Windows accessory.

On-line libraries Provide publications in an electronic form easily accessible to users.

On-line storefront A place on the Web where a company markets its products and services. Also referred to as a cybershop.

Point To move the mouse pointer to position it over an item on the desktop.

Pointers Another term for hypertext links that connect one Web page to another. *See also* Hypertext links.

Posting   The act of sending a message to a newsgroup in response to an article you are reading or by submitting an article of your own. *See also* Newsgroup.

Progress bar   Displays important information about the current operation, such as the percentage loaded of a Web page's layout and graphics. *See also* Load a Web page.

RAM (random access memory)   The memory that can be used by applications to perform necessary tasks while the computer is on. When you turn the computer off, all information in RAM is lost.

Run   To operate a program.

Screen saver   A moving pattern that fills your screen after your computer has not been used for a specified amount of time.

Scroll bar   A bar that appears at the bottom and/or right edge of a window whose contents are not entirely visible. Each scroll bar contains a scroll box and two scroll arrows. You click the arrows or drag the box in the direction you want the window to move.

Scroll box   Located in the vertical and horizontal scroll bars and indicates your relative position in a Web page. *See also* Horizontal scroll bar and Vertical scroll bar.

Search engine   A program that uses entries in a search form to scan for relevant information stored in a search tool. *See also* Search form.

Search form   A Web page that enables you to specify what information a search engine should search for. *See also* Search engine.

Secured site   Refers to any virtual mall or storefront that maintains confidentiality with users who visit it. *See also* Virtual mall and On-line storefront.

Security indicator   A door key icon which indicates if the information you are viewing is secured. If the door key icon displays in blue, then the information is secured; if the door key is broken and displayed in gray, then the Web document is not secured. *See also* Web pages and Web documents.

Select   To highlight, or mark, an item so that a subsequent action can be carried out on the item.

Spider   A program that travels the Web to gather, compile, and index information. A spider indexes the text in Web pages, so it can locate specific Web pages based on their content. This type of search tool uses a search engine to pin-point links to Web pages covering a specific topic. Examples of spiders would be WebCrawler and Jumpstation. *See also* Content-oriented search and Search engine.

Status indicator   The Netscape Corporation company logo that appears in the upper right corner of the screen and animates as a new Web page is loading. When the status indicator stops moving, the page loading process is complete. *See also* Load a Web page.

Strand   A series of linked Web pages. *See also* Hypertext links.

Structuring tag   A type of HTML tag that marks the element of a Web page, such as the title, head, and body. Structuring tags are used to organize the elements of a Web page. *See also* HyperText Markup Language (HTML).

Subject-oriented catalog   A search tool which lists topics alphabetically from A-Z to facilitate browsing. This type of search tool is effective in finding general or broad information. Examples of subject-oriented catalogs would be The WWW Virtual Library at CERN, Yahoo, and Planet Earth. *See also* Subject-oriented search.

Subject-oriented search   Type of search effective in finding general or broad information. *See also* Subject-oriented catalog.

Subscribed   The process of following and participating in a newsgroup discussion. *See also* Newsgroup.

Surfing the Web   Refers to the activity of navigating all the links found in searching for specific Web pages or information on a specific topic. *See also* Hypertext links.

Task List   A window that displays the active applications and programs. You can use the Task List to switch between active applications and programs.

Telnet   An Internet utility that enables you to connect to and use a remote computer.

Telnet client program   An application that enables Netscape to communicate using Telnet to connect to a remote computer. *See also* Telnet.

Text file   A document file containing words, letters, or numbers, but not special computer instructions, such as formatting.

The Web   Another name for the World Wide Web—a vast series of electronic documents called Web pages or Web documents that are linked together over the Internet. Also referred to as WWW and W3. *See also* Web page.

Thread   The flow of conversation in a newsgroup. *See also* Newsgroup.

Tim Berners-Lee   A researcher at the European Particle Physics Laboratory (CERN) in Geneva who deployed the first components of the World Wide Web over the Internet.

Title bar   Displays the title of the current Web page.

Toolbar   Contains icons that function as shortcuts to frequently used Netscape menu commands.

Top level domain   The final three letters of the domain name that indicate the kind of Web site being accessed. *See also* Domain name.

Tour guide   A search tool used to find new, unusual, and outstanding Web pages. Also referred to as guides or travel guides. Examples of tour guides would be Spry City, Global Network Navigator, and Edge of the Web.

Travel guide   A search tool used to find new, unusual, and outstanding Web pages. Also referred to as tour guides or guides. Examples of travel guides would be Spry City, Global Network Navigator, and Edge of the Web.

Tunneling   The process of navigating through the layers of menus in Gopherspace. *See also* Gopherspace.

Unfollowed link   A textual link that appears in blue, indicating you have not yet selected that link. *See also* Hypertext links.

Uniform Resource Locator (URL)   Unique string of text that identifies the location of a Web page on the World Wide Web. Also known as the address for a Web page.

Unsubscribe   The process of removing a newsgroup from your list of available newsgroups. *See also* Newsgroup.

Usenet   A system of over 7,000 newsgroups where Internet users can meet to discuss particular topics. *See also* Newsgroups.

Vertical scroll bar   Allows you to quickly move up and down through a Web page.

Virtual shopping malls   Groups of on-line storefronts where companies market their goods and services on the World Wide Web. *See also* On-line storefront.

Virtual storefront   A Web site established by a corporation wishing to create a unique and individual presence on the Web. For example, companies such as Pizza Hut, Microsoft, Digital Equipment, and IBM have their own individual sites on the Web. *See also* Web site.

W3   Another name for the World Wide Web—a vast series of electronic documents called Web pages or Web documents that are linked together over the Internet. Also referred to as The Web. *See also* Web page.

Web browser   Computer program that enables you to use the World Wide Web to find, load, and view Web pages. Web browsers offer easy-to-use point and click environments for quickly accessing information on the Web. Examples would be Netscape Navigator 1.1 for Windows and Mosaic.

Web document   A specially formatted file designed for use on the World Wide Web that enables you to display information to anyone using the World Wide Web. Web pages typically include text, graphics, and links to other Web pages, and sometimes sound and video clips. Also referred to as a Web page. *See also* Hypertext link.

Web page   A specially formatted file designed for use on the World Wide Web that enable you to display information to anyone using the World Wide Web. Web pages typically include text, graphics, and links to other Web pages, and sometimes sound and video clips. Also referred to as Web documents. *See also* Hypertext links.

Web server   A computer that makes Web pages available to World Wide Web users. Also referred to as a Web site.

Web site   A computer that makes Web pages available to World Wide Web users. Also referred to as a Web server.

Window   A rectangle space on a screen in which a program or application runs.

World Wide Web (WWW)   A vast series of electronic documents called Web Pages or Web Documents that are linked together over the Internet. Also referred to as The Web and W3. *See also* Web page.

WWW Illustrated On-line Companion   An extensive guide to sites on the Web designed to be used in concert with this text.

WWW Virtual Library at CERN   Largest subject-oriented catalog on the Web covering a wide range of subjects. *See also* Subject-oriented catalog.

Index